Post-Soviet Legacies and Conflicting Values in Europe

Russian, Eurasian, and Eastern European Politics

Series Editor: Michael O. Slobodchikoff, Troy University

Mission Statement

Following the collapse of the Soviet Union, little attention was paid to Russia, Eastern Europe, and the former Soviet Union. The United States and many Western governments reassigned their analysts to address different threats. Scholars began to focus much less on Russia, Eastern Europe and the former Soviet Union, instead turning their attention to East Asia among other regions. With the descent of Ukraine into civil war, scholars and governments have lamented the fact that there are not enough scholars studying Russia, Eurasia, and Eastern Europe. This series focuses on the Russian, Eurasian, and Eastern European region. We invite contributions addressing problems related to the politics and relations in this region. This series is open to contributions from scholars representing comparative politics, international relations, history, literature, linguistics, religious studies, and other disciplines whose work involves this important region. Successful proposals will be accessible to a multidisciplinary audience, and advance our understanding of Russia, Eurasia, and Eastern Europe.

Advisory Board

Books in the Series

Post-Soviet Legacies and Conflicting Values in Europe

Generation *WhY*?

Lena M. Surzhko-Harned
and Ekaterina Turkina

LEXINGTON BOOKS
Lanham • Boulder • New York • London

Published by Lexington Books
An imprint of The Rowman & Littlefield Publishing Group, Inc.
4501 Forbes Boulevard, Suite 200, Lanham, Maryland 20706
www.rowman.com

Unit A, Whitacre Mews, 26-34 Stannary Street, London SE11 4AB

British Library Cataloguing in Publication Information Available

Library of Congress Cataloging-in-Publication Data Available

ISBN 978-1-4985-3197-9 (cloth : alk. paper)
ISBN 978-1-4985-3198-6 (electronic)

♾TM The paper used in this publication meets the minimum requirements of American National Standard for Information Sciences—Permanence of Paper for Printed Library Materials, ANSI/NISO Z39.48-1992.

Printed in the United States of America

To our parents and grandparents, with love and gratitude.

Contents

Series Foreword

Generational Change: Competing Identities in Postcommunist States

Following the collapse of the Soviet Union, little attention was paid to Russia, Eastern Europe, and the former Soviet Union. The United States and many Western governments reassigned their analysts to address different threats. Scholars began to focus much less on Russia, Eastern Europe, and the former Soviet Union, instead turning their attention to East Asia among other regions. With the descent of Ukraine into civil war, scholars and governments have lamented the fact that there are not enough scholars studying Russia, Eurasia, and Eastern Europe. Scholars must again turn their focus on this extremely important geographic area. There remains much misunderstanding about the politics of the region. With tensions between governments at heightened levels unprecedented since the Cold War, scholarship addressing the politics of the region is extremely vital. The Russian, Eurasian, and Eastern European Politics Book Series aims at remedying the deficiency in the study and understanding of the politics of Eurasia.

The transition from communism to capitalism has been very difficult for many Eastern European states. Some of the states have been much more successful in their economic and political transitions than other states. While the process of democratic transition was widely studied in the 1990s, few scholars have examined the effect that generational change would have on the postcommunist states. A new generation is starting to come to power that never experienced communism, causing a tension with the previous generation. This tension between generations presents a very difficult dilemma for postcommunist states as they continue the process of transformation. This book examines generational difference and their effects on political change in postcommunist states. This is an extremely important topic, and this book should be required reading for all political scientists who study political transition.

Michael O. Slobodchikoff
Series Editor
Lexington Russian, Eurasian and Eastern European Politics Book Series

Preface

When we first started to discuss this project in 2007 we had very little idea how poignant our research will become ten years later. We were graduate students at the University of Pittsburgh. Ekaterina, a native of Russian Federation, and Lena, a native of Ukraine, both pursued our PhDs and worked at the European Union Center of Excellence at the University Center for International Studies. At the time our curiosity was matched by our idealism and optimism. The study of democratization, market economic relations, European integration, and nationalism attracted us both due to, in many respects, as we later admitted to each other, our experiences with the post-Soviet transition of the 1990s.

While we shared a common language and arguably had very similar childhood experiences, we were acutely aware of the different impacts that the post-Soviet transition left on our home countries. Yet, we also realized that our generation both profited and was shaped by the process of economic and political transition. While we saw firsthand the physical and psychological effects that the aftermath of the regime collapse left on the people of older generations, we felt that our experience with the transition, which coincided with the formative decade of our lives, left a profound impact on our worldviews, which differed from our parents and grandparents. More of us had a chance to travel abroad. We had chewing gum and jeans readily available to us. We consumed more Western culture than was good for us, according to our elders. We profited from expanding globalization in telecommunication technology, and more of us were fluently multilingual. Thus, we set out to seek empirical validation to our claim that the postcommunist generation stood apart from the previous generation.

Among the casual conversations of scholars of postcommunist transition, one can frequently hear a suggestion, if not an assertion, that failures or shortcomings of political democratic transition in the former Soviet Union had much to do with the lack in democratic values and experiences among the leadership and the population. To put it more scientifically, the post-Soviet political culture did not allow for democratic consolidation. The only hope of a solution to this problem would be if the new post-Soviet generation can grow up to manifest the democratic values and contribute to the consolidation of the democratic transition which started in the 1990s. The political activism and the so-called colored revolutions of the 2000s seem to validate this point, as more members of the post-Soviet generation across the post-Soviet space asserted their right to, and desire to, break with Soviet style leadership and old structures. Unfortunately, the revolutions did not seem to produce the desired or even intended effects. Yet, they seem to have laid the path for a future manifestation of political unrest spearheaded by this younger generation.

The 2011–2012 anti-corruption protests in Russia and the 2013 Euromaidan seemed once again to highlight the generational divide in and across these societies. In Russia, the demonstrations and protests, while a challenge to the system, did not result in revolution. In Ukraine, on the other hand, Euromaidan turned into the Revolution of Dignity, which resulted in the flight and abdication of power by the sitting president Yanukovych. The revolution ushered a new era in Ukrainian political reality, which included Russian annexation of Crimea and war in Donbas region. These events proved sobering and informative. In our research, we sought to understand these events through the perspective of generational conflict and while we fully understand the complexity of the situation, we remain optimistic that it is within the power and will of the new generation of post-Soviet citizens to be a part of the solution.

In the interest of full disclosure, we must admit that we share a healthy dose of disagreement when it comes to the current geopolitical situation around the world and in our own neighborhood. Yet, we feel that at the times of heated political rhetoric, propaganda, miscommunication, and misinformation, we academics, nay all thinking persons of the world, must engage in meaningful and respectful dialogue, continue to rely on facts, and seek scientific knowledge. We know that some of our assertions and conclusions will not be popular with everyone, yet, scientific research is not done for the sake of popularity. In the following pages, we sought to lay out the questions we found fascinating, both personally and professionally, and provide answers we found in a decade of research.

In conducting this research, we could not have done without the help of dedicated friends and colleagues, who have read and reread our drafts, listened to our ideas, and offered constructive criticism and guidance. We would like to express our deep gratitude to Kostas Kourtikakis, Galina Zapryanova,

Evgeny Postnikov, Elena Berezkina, Caitlin Handerhan, Klara Wisniewska, Verna Ehret, and Aude Le Cottier. Our work would not be possible without the financial and logistical support of Mercyhurst University, HEC Montreal, the European Union Studies Center and Center for Russian and Eastern European Studies, and the University Center for International Studies at the University of Pittsburgh.

On a personal note, we would like to thank our families. To our parents and grandparents, the generations who have come before us, we are indebted to you for making us who we are today. To our spouses we are grateful for the love and support you offered to us throughout this journey. To the generations who will succeed us, we hope to leave this world for you a better place than we found it.

Lena Surzhko-Harned and Ekaterina Turkina
August 2017

Introduction

Postcommunist Transition and Conflict in Europe

The postcommunist transition in Europe is generally viewed as one of the most important and complicated transformations in modern history. In addition to political, economic, and institutional shifts, the continent's social structure underwent tremendous changes as a result of the transitional processes. Yet, as the experience of post-Soviet years have shown, the societies of the postcommunist states are far from monolithic and homogenous when it comes to politics and economics, and, moreover, these societies did not follow the same post-transitional template.

A conflict between Ukraine and Russia became one of the most significant in a line of conflicts between Russia and the former republics of the Soviet Union, which unfolded in the beginning of the twenty-first century. The conflict between Moscow and Kyiv raises important questions from the perspectives of foreign policy and international relations, as well as from the perspective of a sociological study of transitions and regime changes. It has been suggested that the conflict is an outgrowth of postcommunist transition and the changes in societal experiences and values in the past twenty years (Riabchuk, 2015; Kuzio, 2015). Yet, to date, the empirical evidence of these assertions is rather weak. This book presents a unique and rigorous study, which focuses on the effects that politico-economic regime change has had on the socioeconomic and political values among transitional societies. It also examines the vectors of post-transitional politico-economic policies taken by these societies in light of these value changes.

A special attention is paid to the generational differences between and within the postcommunist states. We pay special attention to the generation whose socialization period—the term widely used in sociological and socio-psychological literature to denote teenage years (Mishler & Rose, 2007; Searing, Schwartz, & Lind, 1973)—coincided with the period of political

transition in the wake of the collapse of the Soviet Union. The special focus
on the transitional generation is intentional. The persons who were teens
during the politico-economic transition of late 1980s and 1990s are now
approaching the productive and politically active decades of their lives.
These are the persons who shall shape the future political landscape of the
post-communist world; therefore, a better understanding of this generation
is in order. We expect that the transition had an important impact on sociopolitical views and core personal values, including attitudes toward authority, state and economic competition, the importance of individual freedoms
and responsibilities, personal independence, etc. In this book, we argue that
the dramatic effects of postcommunist transition, coupled with turbulence
of teenage years, produced lasting effects on these individuals that set them
apart from previous generations raised in the same socio-political system of
the Soviet Union.

It has become conventional to refer to this early wave of millennials as
Generation Y. Our title is a play on words that includes this conventional title
as well as a deep existential question that is persistent among the representatives of this generation—why? As we discover thoughout this book, persons
of the Generation Y are deeply skeptical of conventional wisdoms, idioms,
and absolutes accepted by their parents and grandparents. The collapse of the
previous system and the authoritative institutions of the Soviet Union, newly
found freedoms of democratization and market economic forces, and changes
in geopolitical order all had profound impact on Generation "WhY."

The constructivist approach to international relations suggests that societal
values influence the domestic and foreign policy choices of the state. This
book adopts the constructivist approach and argues that current politico-economic trajectories pursued by the post-communist Europe are influenced by
the value systems developed over the past twenty years. The transitional process, which included the collapse of the Soviet Union, political and economic
reforms, and the prospect of integration with the European Union, has had a
lasting effect on the politico-economic structure of postcommunist Europe.
The book makes a special effort to explain the current Russian-Ukrainian
crisis using the value-based and generational perspective.

This introductory chapter lays out the major theoretical assumption and
assertions underpinning the empirical explorations presented in this study.

POST-COMMUNIST TRANSITION AND
SHIFTING VALUES IN EUROPE

Our analytical framework is inspired by and takes its intellectual root in
the seminal work of Inglehart and Welzel (2005). In their *Modernization,*

Cultural Change, and Democracy: The Human Development Sequence, Inglehart and Welzel argue that there is an ongoing trend in cultural value changes around the world. Relying on an expanded conception of Maslow's hierarchy of needs, they argue that the economic growth and democratization that accompany modernization lead to a shift in cultural values along two dimensions: traditional vs. secular values, and survival vs. self-expressive values. Securing economic stability leads to the systemic satisfaction of the survival needs. At this point, people are free to move up the Maslow's hierarchy of needs and develop the postmodernist values of self-expression.

In their analysis of global trends, Inglehart and Welzel find that there are important differences in traditional vs. secular values and survival vs. self-expressive values among the "Western" and postcommunist European states. In their view, there appears to be a general move toward post-materialism in Western Europe, and differences between generations are insignificant (Inglehart & Welzel, 2005). However, matters are quite different when it comes to postcommunist societies, in which generational differences are greater than in Western Europe, in that the older generations are more inclined toward traditional values. Nevertheless, it is expected that over time with economic growth and modernization, all the generations in postcommunist societies will gradually shift toward postmodern values (Inglehart & Welzel, 2005).

We suggest that value changes take place along three interrelated yet distinct dimensions: economic attitudes, political attitudes (such as support for democratic governance), and deep cultural values (traditional vs. secular values and survival vs. self-expressive values). Economic attitudes stem from security in the competitive world of a market economy (Kitschelt, 1992, 1995, 2000). Support for democratic governance involves a basic understanding of and support for democratic institutions. Finally, secular and self-expressive values, such as attitudes toward minorities and women's rights, require a deeper societal shift that accompanies politico-economic changes. In our view, these value changes occur gradually over time and move through each of these phases in a successive manner. Figure I.1 depicts this gradual process graphically.

Since the transition has taken place relatively recently, most of our analysis is concerned primarily with the first two rungs of this value ladder.[1] We contend that the development of emancipatory values in these populations will occur over a longer period. Thus, for the majority of the analyses presented here we are concerned with attitudes in politico-economic realms, namely, the following five arenas: attitudes toward democracy, attitudes toward state ownership of businesses, attitudes toward income inequality, economic competition, and state interference in socioeconomic affairs. However, we make several detours into the development of the so-called emancipatory values and the role of the European Union in fostering these values in Eastern Europe.

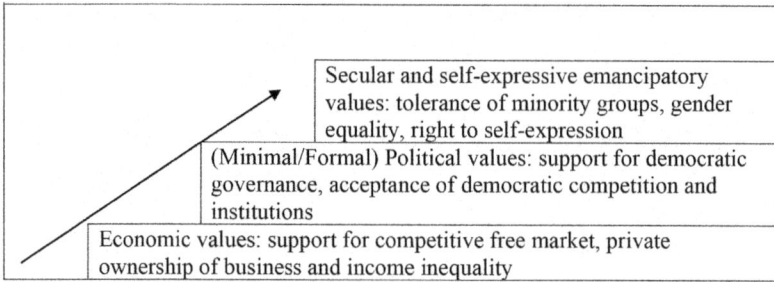

Figure I.1   **Gradual Value Change in Post-Communist Societies.** Created by the authors.

Generation "WhY?"

The sociological theory of generations and social change introduced by Karl Mannheim (1952) and developed by a series of authors (Alwin & McCammon, 2003; Dunham, 1998; Edmunds & Turner, 2002) provides a framework for the examination of social, cultural, economic, and political change as experienced by the people of different generations. The term "generation" refers to the people born at around the same time and therefore experienced historical events at around the same time in their lives. This generational perspective stipulates that there is always a difference in values and perceptions among generations, which is framed as a "generation conflict." It is generally assumed that generations that are temporally closer to each other are supposed to have a higher convergence of norms, ideals, and beliefs than generations further apart from each other. However, some studies find that history sometimes offers so-called "turning points" among generations—or, in other words, cataclysmic events so profound that even generations that are close to each other might have significant differences in norms, values, perceptions, and life (e.g., Strauss and Howe (1991).

In the case of the postcommunist societies, we postulate that the transition should have had a profound effect on generational differences. Thus, we expect that two consecutive generations that are raised in different political, economic, and social regimes should be more different from one another in values, norms, and perceptions than generations spaced further apart, but raised in the same politico-economic and ideological system.

While we accept that such tremendous sociopolitical events as the collapse of the Soviet Union and the transition that followed affected all of the citizens of the region, we propose that the children of *perestroika* years were affected somewhat differently than their parents and grandparents. This particular generation can be seen as a bridge or a gap generation, depending on one's point of view, influenced by socialization under the previous communist regime, the liberalization of the reforms, and the transition itself. Thus, numerous and often conflicting ideational forces influenced the development of these individuals.

Strauss and Howe (1991) describe a cyclical theory of history through the lens of repeating generational archetypes. They explore Anglo-American history by dividing it into saecula, or seasonal cycles of history. Such saeculum is about 90 years long (the length of a long human life) and is further divided into four "turnings" that are about 22 years long—as long as the period between birth and adulthood, or a full reproductive cycle. According to this study, children raised during a particular "turning" share similar experiences, resulting in distinct generational types. Strauss and Howe suggest that interactions between generations can help explain why major crises occur roughly every 90 years (e.g., 1773–1861) and why spiritual awakenings recur halfway between those crises. We suggest that, in addition to endogenous factors related to specificities of generations and interactions between generations (generational conflict), there are important exogenous factors, such as major geopolitical and economic changes, predetermining the generational "turning" points. For instance, Strauss and Howe's generational approach combined with consideration of macroeconomic and political factors can help explain the collapse of the communist regime and the following post-communist transformation: the communist system existed for roughly 70 years (average life span) and collapsed at the "turning point" when the global and regional politico-economic forces, combined with historical formation of the new generation, led to major systemic shifts.

Modeling Generations

Relying on the theoretical framework developed by Strauss and Howe (1991), who explore Anglo-American history through four generational cycles (or "turnings"), we distinguish between four major "turnings" in the history of the selected countries between 1902 and 1990. The turnings also coincide with the biological reproductive generational cycle of a little over twenty years (Alwin & McCammon, 2003).

The first "turning" is associated with the turbulent revolutionary period at the beginning of the twentieth century, which included the formation of the Soviet Union and the First World War, and which affected all the countries selected for analysis. Our first generational group is thus defined as the people born between 1909 and 1930. This generation was very influenced by the political and economic instability of those years.

The second "turning" is associated with the Second World War, the war period itself and immediate postwar aftereffects. As such, this generation includes people born between 1931 and 1951. This generation is deeply affected by the destruction caused by the war as well as the postwar period of reconstruction and hope.

The third "turning" includes people whose childhood and adolescence coincided with the development of the Eastern Block, including the Warsaw Treaty, the development of the COMECON (Council for Mutual Economic Assistance), and the so-called "golden years" of the Soviet Union. Specifically, we are referring here to the progressive years of *shestidesyatye* and the political stability of the early *zastoi*. Thus, we place this generation in the 20-year period between 1952 and 1972.

The fourth "turning" consists of people whose birth and adolescence occurred between 1973 and 1990. This last generation is characterized by its members' unique experience of the political, economic, and social transition instigated by the fall of the Berlin Wall, the dissolution of the Soviet Union, the integration into the world economy and globalization, and orientation toward the European integration of former communist Central and Eastern European countries. In the following statistical tables, we refer to these generations as generation 1, 2, 3, and 4, respectively.

Data and Analysis

The analysis employed in this book relies on a mixed methodology. It incorporates quantitative and qualitative methods. The statistical analyses of large N data are based on the World Values Survey data. World Values Survey is a global network of social scientists studying changing values and their impact on social and political life, led by an international team of scholars, with the WVS association and secretariat headquartered in Stockholm, Sweden.[2] The WVS consists of nationally representative surveys conducted in almost 100 countries which contain almost 90 percent of the world's population, using a common questionnaire. The WVS is the largest noncommercial, cross-national, time-series investigation of human beliefs and values ever executed, currently including interviews with almost 400,000 respondents. The WVS seeks to help scientists and policy makers to understand changes in the beliefs, values, and motivations of people throughout the world. Thousands of political scientists, sociologists, social psychologists, anthropologists, and economists have used the data to analyze such topics as economic development, democratization, religion, gender equality, social capital, and subjective well-being. The data have also been widely used by government officials, journalists, students, and groups at the World Bank, which have analyzed the linkages between cultural factors and economic development.

We also use in-depth interviews that we conducted between 2007 and 2016, as well as experimental surveys conducted in 2013. Each chapter spells out the particular methodology applied therein.

Outline of the Book

Chapter 1 analyzes post-Soviet transition and domestic variations in value systems between the generations of post-Soviet countries. Focusing on generational trends in Belarus, Russia, and Ukraine with a special focus on the "transitional" generation of 1990s, the chapter evaluates sociopolitical values among different generations of post-Soviet citizens through the lens of regime change. The results indicate that two consecutive generations raised in different regimes differ more in values than generations further apart yet raised in the same politico-economic system. The chapter provides an in-depth analysis of this generation gap phenomenon. The highlight of the chapter consists of interviews with the members of the transitional generation and their personal experiences of the transition.

Chapter 2 takes a broad look at the postcommunist transition by analyzing a wide range of postcommunist states and incorporating the effects of the European integration. The chapter explores the effects of postcommunist transition and European enlargement on intergenerational politico-economic values in three groups of countries: Central and Eastern European countries that became European Union members; countries with EU membership prospects; and those that have no membership prospects, at least in the foreseeable future. The analysis indicates considerable differences between these three groups of countries and shows that over time, Europeanization served as an intra-cohort mechanism of social change: it smoothed over intergenerational differences and led to a trend of convergence in values between new Eastern members of the European Union and Western Europe. Europeanization also appears to have some harmonizing power on intergenerational differences in countries with EU-membership prospects. At the same time, the rough postcommunist transition process and the lack of consolidation mechanisms created considerable intergenerational differences in European countries without EU membership prospects, as revealed by the dominance of cohort replacement mechanism in these countries.

Chapter 3 further explores the effect of the European Union on the value changes in postcommunist Europe. The chapter takes a closer look at the possible effect of promised European integration on the changes of domestic values in Ukraine. The soft power of the European Union has been recognized as one of the greatest assets of EU foreign policy. Through treaties of association and trade agreements, the European Union has been shown to influence institutional and policy changes in nonmember states. Yet, there is relatively little analysis of the European Union's power to influence the attitudes and values of individual citizens. This chapter looks at the supranational norm diffusion by exploring attitudes toward LGBT rights in Ukraine. Changes in domestic attitudes are usually attributed to the work of domestic activists and institutions. However, international organizations interested in facilitating positive change in Eastern Europe have been keen on promoting and funding such activities. A survey experiment using media frames was conducted in the spring of 2013, and results are used to compare the ability of the European Union and the ability of domestic political activists to influence attitudes on LGBT rights in Ukraine. The fundamental question the chapter seeks to answer is this: how potent is the soft power of the European Union in introducing value change in the EU neighborhood?

Chapter 4 shift gears from the influence of the supranational institutions and value diffusion and turns to the immediate value conflict between Russia and Ukraine. The chapter examines the conflict through the experiences of the members of the transitional (perestroika) generation to further reveal important divergences in norms and values and important differences in the perception of the conflict. This chapter also places the Russia-Ukraine relationship in a broader normative and geopolitical discourse of the Russia-West (EU/US) relationship and discusses the clash of civilizations from the value-based perspective.

Chapter 5 applies social network analysis (SNA) to explore changes in the social structures connecting Russian and Ukrainian societies from political networks to business networks. The analysis presented in this chapter takes a specific look at the implications of the postcommunist transition for the politico-economic trajectories of post-Soviet Russia and Ukraine. The past few years have proven to be one of the most trying and defining experiences in the two countries' interactions since the collapse of the Soviet Union in 1991. In light of numerous commonalities in cultural values, tight connections between social, business, and politico-economic elites, and strong familial ties between the two societies, the current conflict presents the most intriguing case study in the divergence of the politico-economic values that developed during the transition.

The concluding chapter summarizes the major finding of the previous chapters and positions these findings in the context of the broader literature on regime change, postcommunist transition, globalization, and European integration. Furthermore, the chapter discusses prospects for peace and stability in Europe.

In writing this book, we sought to place the analysis conducted in it in a strong theoretical foundation followed by a rigorous and original analysis using comprehensive methodology. While we are sure that the academic audiences will find our analysis insightful and useful, we also hope that this book will be of interest to general public, because it helps to understand important current events such as the Russia-Ukrainian conflict, European integration and its transformative nature, Russia-EU tensions, as well as generational conflict on post-Soviet space. Moreover, the revealing and colorful accounts of transitional experience through the eyes of real people make the following narrative engaging and utterly human.

NOTES

1. We will analyze the value changes on the remaining steps in subsequent research.

2. www.worldvaluessurvey.org

Chapter 1

A Generation Apart

How the Postcommunist Transition Shaped the Post-Soviet Values

An important aspect of regime transition is change in the system of values, which underpins broader patterns of socioeconomic and political change. In the contemporary world, economy and politics became significantly more complex and can be characterized by intense multilevel processes. The collapse of the Soviet Union and forces of globalization in different sectors and spheres of social, political, and economic activity enhanced the rapid growth of international and transnational linkages, which created economic and political interdependence and led to a dramatic increase in the frequency of flows of capital, labor, and trade across the boundaries of nation-states. The power of national governments became significantly challenged by the new powerful actors such as international organizations, transnational corporations, nongovernmental organizations, terrorist networks, and a variety of regional and global institutions. According to Rosenau (1992), there is a bifurcation of global political and economic systems where an emerging complex, autonomous, multicentric world competes with the long-standing state-centric world of sovereign states.

After the collapse of the Soviet Union, the restructuring of the existing politico-economic regime, geopolitical shifts, reconsideration of territorial boundaries, and opening of the borders allowed for intensified interactions of broader publics and created new patterns in the movement of capital, goods, and services in Eastern Europe. This led to a diffusion of norms, ideas, expectations, and resources across borders and had a significant impact on people's values, beliefs, and perceptions. While there have been studies that explored the effects of postcommunist transition on people's norms, beliefs, and perceptions (Reisinger, Miller, Hesli, & Maher, 1994), few analyses focused on norms and values from the perspective of generations. Mishler and Rose (2007) used time-series data from the New Russia Barometer to analyze the political learning among generations and found that older generations were more supportive of the previous communist regime, while younger generations were more inclined to learn about more participatory forms of political engagement. At the same time, in addition to political attitudes it is important to see if there are generational differences in other important values related to work, economy, and personality traits, as well as to explain existing differences.

To begin our analysis of postcommunist transition and its effect on society, we turn to the detailed evaluation of political views and values among different generations in three post-Soviet Eastern European countries: Belarus, Russia, and Ukraine. We chose to analyze these three Slavic states for the sake of simplicity. The cultural and historical connections between these three reduce the number of extraneous variation and allow for a more streamlined analysis.

Postcommunist transition received a great deal of scholarly attention from a multitude of disciplines. This chapter explores the broader literature on postcommunist transition and outlines the main interdisciplinary arguments about the effects of postcommunist transition on the broader society and public.

Our empirical analysis relies on a two-pronged approach utilizing the quantitative and qualitative methods of data analysis and explores the generational gap in post-Soviet states. We use the World Values Survey data from 1989 to 2008 and in-depth interviews conducted by the authors during the years 2007 to 2016. Given the special focus of this inquiry, we have interviewed individuals whose socialization period coincided with the years immediately following the collapse of the Soviet Union, namely the 1990s.

Following the theory of generations outlined in the previous chapter, we expect to find sharp intergenerational difference prompted by the postcommunist transition. Namely, we expect that Generation "WhY" stands apart from the previous generations. Our analysis goes beyond the examination of sociological differences among generations. This study places the theory of generations in a broader economic and political context and indicates that two consecutive generations raised in different politico-economic regimes exhibit more differences in values and perceptions than generations further apart that were raised in the same politico-economic and ideological system. We call this phenomenon a "generational gap," which is considered to be a significant variable in explaining the gap, or transition period, that was created in between two different politico-economic systems—communism and a market-based economy.

THE STUDY OF TRANSITIONS

Economists, policy analysts, sociologists, and political scientists have analyzed various facets of the postcommunist transition in Eastern Europe. In this section, we attempt to highlight the main arguments of the scholarly community regarding the effect of the economic, political, and sociocultural liberalizing reform on the broader society and public. Thus, we make a case for a necessity of intergenerational analysis of the transition effects.

Economists have been mostly interested in analyzing the ineffectiveness of the economic reform and the results of macroeconomic strategies (Bartlett, 1996; Kornai, Haggard, & Kaufman, 2001), and political economy scholars explored the effects of transformations on political and economic outcomes (Bunce, 1999; Glinavos, 2010; Papava, 2003, 2005). These scholars focused on explaining economic hardships of the 1990s, such as the drop in macroeconomic indicators, the decline of living standards, etc.

The political science and social analyses of postcommunist transition have been mainly preoccupied with explaining variance in democratization policies and the analysis of institutional and social changes (Habermas, 2003; Kopstein & Reilly, 2000; Krasteva & Privitera, 2006; Lankina & Getachew, 2006; Saivetz & Jones, 1994; Schmitter, 2001). With the collapse of the Soviet Union, the entire configuration of institutions that shaped the transitioning countries was expected to change rapidly. Even though this change was desirable in many regards, much hardship has accompanied the radical transformation that followed. Newly discovered political pluralism led to the creation of numerous political parties, which often did not prescribe to ideological dimensions but rather relied on populist and ethno-nationalist rhetoric and single-issue campaign strategies, further undermining democratic consolidation (Alonso & Ruiz-Rufino, 2007; Linz & Stepan, 1996; Mansfield & Snyder, 1995, 2002, 2005; Sakwa, 2008; Snyder, 2000; White, 2000).

Many scholars argue that institutional change has a very important strategic role in transition processes and should occur prior to liberalization, marketization, economic restructuring, and substantial privatization (Elliott, 1997). Therefore, the failure of broader economic initiatives has been partially attributed to the absence of the necessary legal and institutional structures, the enormous destruction of physical and social capital, and the inefficiencies of the third sector, the low level of civil society development and the lack of public-private-third sector coordination mechanisms (Kopstein & Reilly 2000; Lankina & Getachew 2006). Policy analysts examined postcommunist transition by analyzing factors accounting for changes in specific policy sectors (Bachev, 2008; Enev, 2006).

Sociological and cultural accounts of postcommunist transition—our main focus—have focused on the effect of liberalizing reforms on social stratification, social relations, and societal and organizational culture (Grusky, 1994; Kennedy, 2002; King, 2002; King & Szelenyi, 2001; Wesolowski, 1994). Sociological analyses claim that the major effects of transition were the sudden and dramatic changes in inequality, class divergence, and stratification of societies in post-Soviet transition economies that have created serious concerns for the fragile political, economic, and social structures undergoing transformation (Kitschelt, 1992, 1995). The stratification of societies in newly formed democracies and market-based economies contributed to the significant social disappointment and dissatisfaction with the new capitalist and democratic systems, despite the fact that the majority of the population had been ready for significant changes and for a major restructuring of the existing regime. Even though scholars that wrote in the early 1990s claimed that a political culture had developed in post-Soviet states that is receptive to democracy and would sustain democratic institutions and processes (Duch, 1995; Finifter & Mickiewicz, 1992; Gibson, Duch, & Tedin, 1992), later analyses (Fleron, 1996) are less optimistic and explain decreasing support for the concept of democracy by perceived growth of social inequality as a result of market reforms. Sociologists exploring social networks (Ledeneva, 2004) argue that social stratification led to the perseverance of networks serving the economy of favors in postcommunist societies. These networks required constant maintenance and investment, bringing high implicit costs to the state. The closed membership of these networks tended to limit individual action and created lock-in effects for society. These networks often exemplified the negative effects of social capital and had a negative effect on the stability and structure of the political and economic structures of the state. Cultural and anthropological accounts of transition (Humphrey, 1991, 2002) indicate that these networks serving the economy of favors and social stratification had important cultural effects, such as the emergence of consumption culture and individualistic values promoted by the young and wealthy "new Russians." In Humphrey's terminology, new Russians are "new" because they do not support various hoary Soviet values (e.g., the value of supporting the *kollektiv*, the value of production of goods for the benefit of society as a whole).

Even though some scholars argue that regional variation can have an effect on support for political reforms (Finifter, 1996), most researchers believe that politico-economic transformation of the 1990s produced similar macroeconomic effects on all the regions and ethnicities (Lankina & Getachew, 2006). Therefore, despite certain regional and ethnic variation in the three countries under analysis and some interethnic tensions fueled by the transition (e.g., Slavs and Crimean Tatars in Ukraine, Slavs and Caucasus minorities in Russia, etc.), it is legitimate to analyze the effects of the transition on the population-level values. There is also an important argument in the literature that socioeconomic variables have a stronger impact on the formation of certain values (e.g., work attitudes or attitudes to state and economy) than ethnicity (Inkeles & Bauer, 1959).

The interdisciplinary literature review shows that the transitional roller coaster of the successes and failures of the reforms have had a profound impact on the population in general and, as we argue, on those members of the society whose socialization period coincided with the transitional decade. In the following section, we turn to the discussion of the generational gap perspective and our argument regarding the effects of postcommunist transition on the values and attitudes of Generation "WhY."

ANALYZING THE "GENERATION GAP"

This chapter includes two interrelated tracks of analysis. First, logistic regression analysis is applied to the pooled World Values Survey(WVS) data to analyze the generational trends in sociopolitical values between 1989 and 2008. Generations are modeled here based on the theoretical framework developed by Strauss and Howe (1991) and described in detail in the introductory chapter of this book. The model estimates the log likelihood of attitudinal and value subscription among the members of different generations of Soviet citizens. This analysis is employed in order to illustrate the differences between the generations. The second track of our analysis relies on an evaluation of in-depth interviews of those members of the population whose socialization period coincided with the years of transitional change.

The interviews provide fascinating detail regarding the human experiences of transition. They also offer an invaluable insight into the process of political change though the eyes of teenagers, who had little concept of the magnitude of the events they witnessed and yet whose effects they would feel for the rest of their lives. The interviews were conducted in a semi-structured format consisting of a set of core questions supplemented by an in-depth discussion about different subjects the respondent was willing to provide further detail about (Appendix A presents the questionnaire). Each interview focused on the questions related to the particular experience of a respondent in dealing with social, political, and economic aspects of the 1990s, yet went beyond these questions to address broader questions about transition processes, the collapse of the old regime, and the formation of the new regime.

All the interviews were taken in the Russian language and were translated into English. The Appendix A contains the questionnaire that was used for this analysis and Appendix B offers descriptive information on the interviewees. The interviewees provide invaluable insight into the complexities of post-Soviet transition and their effects on the lives of the interviewees. The perceptions of teenagers of such cataclysmic events is often very different from the perceptions of adults. We sought to allow these voices to be heard. This two-prong approach relies on quantitative and qualitative methodological approaches to produce truly insightful results by combining statistical rigor with rich detail of personal experiences communicated in the

interviews to analyze the transitional effect on the generational value differences in post-Soviet societies. The study also situates this qualitative change
in broader national and regional contexts and concludes with prospects for
regional development.

Given our theoretical framework, we expect several outcomes. We expect
to find gaps in attitudes among all four generations. We also expect that
economic and political transition impacted all four generations. However,
the fourth generation should be impacted differently, albeit profoundly, by
the transition, given the impressionable young age of these persons. We now
turn to the empirical data in order to illustrate these hypothesized trends with
the statistical analysis.

INTERGENERATIONAL GAP: QUANTITATIVE ANALYSIS

The goal of the statistical section of this chapter is to show the differences in
values and attitudes among the four generations of Soviet citizens. The WVS
incorporates numerous tools that allow us to tap into these broad spheres. In
our analysis of generational values differences, we focus on two categories
of values. The first category includes general attitudes toward political and
economic relationships. Here we are interested in citizens' attitudes toward
the role of the state in economics and resource distribution, income inequality associated with market transition, and democracy as the preferred form
of governance. The second category includes the individual personal values.
We conceptualize personal values as those that include character traits that
persons find most desirable or important.

The WVS questionnaire includes a question that asks the respondents to
identify those qualities that should be encouraged in children. The respondents have an opportunity to identify up to five traits that they value most.
These traits include independence, hard work, feeling of responsibility,
imagination, tolerance and respect for other people, thrift, determination and
perseverance, religious faith, unselfishness, and obedience. By analyzing the
traits one most hopes to see nurtured in children, we can gain a great perspective on the personal values of the individual respondent.

We are interested in the evaluation of the personal values of individuals
because inadvertently we expect that these values are interconnected with
the broader attitudes toward state and economics. As the results of Pearson's
correlations, depicted in Table 1.1, suggest, holding certain personal characteristics as important corresponds to particular views about the role of state
and economic relations. Thus, the support for a strong state is highly correlated with values of obedience. On the other hand, independence, personal
responsibility, and tolerance are highly correlated with positive attitudes

Table 1.1 Pearson's Correlations: Personal Characteristics and Attitudes toward State and Economics

	Independence	Hard Work	Responsibility	Imagination	Tolerance
State Ownership	-0.81***	-0.35***	-0.73***	-0.12***	-0.31**
Income Inequality	0.62***	0.28*	0.03	0.08	0.09
State Responsibility	-0.59**	-0.47***	-0.85***	-0.22***	-0.15*
Democracy is Preferred	0.74***	0.25*	0.56**	0.33**	0.68***

Note: *** p<0.01, ** p<0.05, * p<0.1

	Thrift	Determination	Religious faith	Unselfishness	Obedience
State Ownership	-0.59***	-0.10	-0.61***	0.02	0.66***
Income Inequality	0.77***	0.06	0.13	-0.18*	-0.38***
State Responsibility	-0.60**	-0.25*	-0.47**	0.04	0.52***
Democracy is Preferred	0.65***	0.20**	0.03	-0.09	-0.72***

Note: ***p < 0.01, **p < 0.05, *p < 0.1.

toward democracy. The support for income inequality is highly correlated with values of independence and thrift. By focusing on the evaluation of intergenerational differences in these two interrelated categories of values, we hope to elucidate the existing value divergence in post-Soviet space.

In addition to the relationship between the personal values and the attitudes toward the state, we believe that there is a general relationship among the ten characteristics listed above. Table 1.2 represents the results of the exploratory factor analysis of the aforementioned childhood characteristics. The results indicate that the general characteristics appear to load on three distinct factors. Hard work, tolerance and respect for others, thrift, and obedience fall within factor one. Independence, a feeling of personal responsibility, and perseverance load on factor two. Imagination, religious faith, and unselfishness fall within factor three. Based on this analysis, we construct three composite variables, taping in the personal values of respondents. The composite variable, which combines the four characteristics loading on factor one, taps into what we refer to as collectivist values. Obedience, thrift, hard work, and respect for others seem to indicate the preference for a socially minded collectivist person. The characteristics combined in the second composite variable and factor two outline individualistic values, where personal individual freedom and independence are dominant. Finally, our third composite variable taps into what we shall refer to as humanistic values, with the emphasis on unselfishness, faith, and imagination.

We expect that there will be a great deal of generational variation between these three categories of values. Moreover, we expect that the fourth generation holds individualistic values of independence, responsibility, and determination above all others, as compared with their older counterparts. The experience of liberalization and transition would have taught the children of the perestroika period that they must be self-reliant and resourceful in order to succeed in life. The Russian term *"vertetsya,"* literally meaning "to spin,"

Table 1.2   Factor Analysis: Important Child Qualities (Personal Values)

	Factor 1	*Factor 2*	*Factor 3*
Independence	−0.6259	**0.247**	0.0529
Hard Work	**0.4909**	0.1901	−0.1457
Feeling of Responsibility	0.1598	**0.5993**	−0.0117
Imagination	−0.526	−0.1104	**0.0452**
Tolerance and Respect for other people	**0.4918**	0.2207	0.4678
Thrift/Saving Money	0.3717	−0.1869	−0.4811
Determination and Perseverance	−0.3626	**0.4286**	−0.2513
Religious Faith	−0.0718	−0.5356	**0.2357**
Unselfishness	−0.0042	−0.1004	**0.6893**
Obedience	**0.1869**	−0.6011	−0.2906

became the motto of the transitional decade as the entrepreneurially minded individuals sought to carve out their own way at the time of political and economic uncertainty. The political instability showed that reliance on government did not pay off.

To analyze the generational attitudinal differences, we apply the logistic regression model to the pooled data of WVS. Appendix C outlines the exact wording of the WVS survey questions. We choose to employ logit because this model provides us with estimates of the likelihood of identifying one or the other value or attitude as salient. The results are depicted in the form of odds ratios. This allows us to compare them across generations and across values. The dependent variables have been recoded into dichotomous dummy variables. Model coefficients larger than one show the positive effect on the likelihood of the dependent variable value equal to one or occurring, while coefficients smaller than one depict a negative effect on the occurrence likelihood. Generation one is used as a reference category in all of the following analysis. Gender (a dummy variable for female), education levels (measured at three levels—elementary, secondary, and higher), and income (a self-reported level of income ordered in categories from lowest to highest) are used as demographic controls in all of the models. A country-level control variable is also used in the analysis.[1] The time variation is also accounted for by including the wave of interview as a variable in our model. As mentioned above, there are three waves of the interview included in this study: 1989–1993, 1994–1996, and 2005–2007. The estimator of interview waves (scaled as a year count) shows the effects of time, thus eliminating some noise from our results. We also include an interaction between our time estimator and generation variables, which should tap into the overtime changes. We begin with the analysis of the generational differences in personal values by examining the three value categories. We then turn to the analysis of attitudes toward state and economics.

The results of logistic regression of the three value categories presented in Table 1.3 show tremendous intergenerational differences. The most striking of all is the fourth-generation preference for individualist values. Compared with the first generation, the odds ratio of support for individualist values is positive among all three generations. However, the odds ratio of support for individualist values is considerably larger among the fourth generation at 3.94, as compared with its temporally closest third generation at 1.99. These results seem to support our expectations regarding the fourth generation's divergence from the previous generations. As we expected, the individualist values of personal independence and economic freedoms are valued the highest by the fourth generation. Moreover, it appears that the divergence between generation four and generation three is much larger than that between three and two. This finding gives support to our expectation that generations raised

Table 1.3 Intergenerational Differences in Personal Values (Logistic Regression Odds Ratio)

	Collectivist Values (Factor 1)	Individualist Values (Factor 2)	Humanistic Values (Factor 3)
Generational Effects (Generation 1 as base):			
Generation 2	0.71***	1.73***	0.41***
	0.03	0.05	0.04
Generation 3	0.12***	1.99***	0.47***
	0	0.03	0.05
Generation 4	0.13***	3.94***	0.12***
	0.01	0.54	0.02
Demographics:			
Female	1.51	0.82	1.14***
	0.46	0.13	0.03
Level of Education	0.98	1.37***	1.15***
	0.04	0.01	0.04
Income	1.01	1.11***	0.98*
	0.02	0.02	0.01
Russian Federation	2.83***	1.28**	0.77**
	0.17	0.13	0.09
Time Effects:			
Wave of the Interview (Temporal Variations)	0.54***	1.16***	0.89***
	0	0.01	0
Generation 2* Interview Wave	1.14***	0.96***	1.28***
	0.01	0.01	0.02
Generation 3* Interview Wave	1.53***	0.97**	1.25***
	0	0.01	0.02
Generation 4* Interview Wave	1.41***	0.82***	1.70***
	0.02	0.03	0.04
Constant	326.27***	0.95	0.78***
	56.75	0.18	0.05
N	8494	8494	8494
"LL"	855.35	3132.03	5611.24
BIC	1719.74	6273.11	11231.52

Note: $*p < .10, **p < .05, ***p < .01$.

temporally closer together, yet on different sides of transition, are more divergent than those raised temporally further apart but under the same sociopolitical system.

Similar divergence and distance in values appears in the odds ratios of support for humanistic values. The fourth generation seems to value the traits of this composite measure the least as compared with the third and second generation, whose odds ratios again appear to be close in numeric value. The intriguing results of Table 1.3 are the perceptions of collectivist values. It appears that both generation three and generation four are very close in their distinct dislike for the collectivist values as compared with generation two. While all three generations appear to disapprove of the collectivist values as compared with generation one, which is used as a reference, generations three and four have the most disdain. It is not surprising that generation three should dislike the collectivist values; after all, it would be this generation that experienced the hypocrisy and inefficiency of the socialist system during the *zastoi* era. However, unlike the fourth generation, the third generation does not seem to have accepted the alternative individualist values as enthusiastically.

The results of the demographic characteristic also fall in line with the intuitive expectation. It appears that women are more inclined to support the humanistic values, while wealthier persons do not. Individualist values are favored by individuals with higher education and higher incomes. The country variable shows us that in Russia, as compared with the other two republics, the support for collectivist values is the highest. There is also a significant support for individualist values, while the odds ratio for the support of humanistic values is significant and negative. As we mentioned earlier, while we appreciate the value and importance of potential interregional differences, such analysis does not fall within the purview of this inquiry.

The temporal variables show that over time there is a general decrease in the support for humanistic and collectivist values and a general significant increase in the support for individualist values across the board. The odds ratios of the interaction terms show that over time there have been significant changes in the perceptions of collectivist and humanistic values in all generations, while the temporal changes in perceptions of individualist values are low. The results of the analysis presented in Table 1.3 leave us with little doubt that various Soviet generations have very different values. Furthermore, the "generational gap" between the fourth generation and the previous generations sets it further apart.

We now turn to the second step of our analysis, which examines the general attitudes toward political and economic relationships. Here we are interested in people's attitudes toward democracy as a form of the political system, state influence over economic competition, income inequality as a result of economic competition, and state responsibility to provide for those harmed by free market competition. We expect that compared to the three older Soviet generations, the fourth or transitional perestroika generation is predisposed to approve of market economic relations and a democratic form of governance. We expect this because this generation has minimal experience with the previous nondemocratic regime as a framework of reference and therefore is more willing to accept democracy as a legitimate form of governance, unlike the previous generations. Moreover, the economic turmoil affected this generation differently than the rest. As children, these persons would not have a direct firsthand experience with economic hardships, as they would have been provided for by their parents.

Table 1.4 represents the results of the logistic regression analysis of inter-generational differences in respondents' attitudes toward state and economics. Given the aforementioned relationship between personal values and attitudes toward state, we include the three composite value variables into the models. The models also include the temporal variables and the demographic controls, including a country-level control variable for the Russian Federation.

The results presented in Table 1.4 are quite striking. The fourth generation seems to stand out from the previous generations in all the attitudes. While all three generations appear to be considerably less likely than the first generation to support state ownership and state responsibility for resource distribution, the odds ratios for the fourth generation are considerably lower than the odds ratios of the previous generations. The opposite is true when it comes to the support for income inequality and democracy. The fourth generation is most likely to believe that income inequality is positive. This suggests that the members of the fourth generation are more inclined to support the market competition than their elders.

The earlier generations appear to be less supportive of democracy as a preferred political system than the fourth transitional generation. This result supports our expectations and suggests that the fourth generation, which did not have much interaction with the previous political system, is more likely to accept democracy as the only game in town. This finding supports previous scholarship focusing on the support of democracy in postcommunist Europe, which suggests that experience with previous nondemocratic system often serves as a frame of reference when evaluating the new democratic form of governance (Mishler & Rose, 2001a, b; Norris, 1999). The results presented so far support our hypothesis regarding the existence of the generational gaps in the attitudes toward politico-economic structures. Moreover, the fourth generation appears to be quite different from the previous generations, illustrating our expectation about the transitional effects on these persons.

The results of the demographic variables are again not surprising. Women tend to be more supportive of the strong state role in property ownership and resource allocation and least supportive of income inequality. This could be a result of women's experience with the collapse of the regime and removal of the generous welfare net provided by the Soviet Union. The same trends are seen in the persons of lower education and lower income. The persons with higher education and higher income, however, are more likely to support a market economy. Interestingly, however, it is only the persons with high levels of education that seem to have significant positive views of democracy.

Table 1.4   Intergenerational Differences in Attitudes toward State and Economy (Logistic)

	State Ownership	Income Inequality	State Responsibility	Democracy is Preferred
Generational Variations (Generation 1 as base category):				
Generation 2	**0.65***	**2.32***	**0.42***	0.9
	0.02	0.02	0.03	0.22
Generation 3	**0.47***	**2.72***	**0.29***	**1.84***
	0.01	0	0.02	0.38
Generation 4	**0.19***	**3.32***	**0.07***	**5.92***
	0.01	0.84	0.02	2.96
Demographics:				
Female	**1.35***	**0.90***	**1.22***	1.04
	0	0.04	0.08	0.16
Level of Education	**0.68***	**1.37***	**0.82***	**1.36****
	0.01	0.1	0.02	0.18
Income	**0.97****	**1.08***	**0.95***	1.02
	0.01	0.02	0.01	0.03
Russia	**2.00***	0.73	0.93	**0.41****
	0.01	0.18	0.27	0.17
Personal Values:				
Collectivist Values	**1.60***	**0.87***	**1.66***	0.96
	0	0.07	0.06	0.24
Individualist Values	**0.71***	1.09	**0.90***	**1.31***
	0.05	0.09	0.03	0.03
Humanistic Values	**0.71****	0.87	**0.80****	1.18
	0.11	0.12	0.07	0.16
Time Effects:				
Wave of the Interview (Temporal Variations)	**1.71***	**1.19***	**0.86***	**1.45***
	0.01	0.03	0.02	0.05
*Generation 2*Interview Wave*	**1.03***	**0.82***	**1.19***	0.99
	0.01	0.02	0.04	0.04
*Generation 3*Interview Wave*	**0.99***	**0.85***	**1.22***	**0.85***
	0	0.02	0.04	0.02
*Generation 4*Interview Wave*	**1.11***	**0.81***	**1.60***	**0.68***
	0.01	0.06	0.11	0.05
Constant	**0.65***	**0.33***	**13.53***	**0.51****
	0.02	0.11	1.1	0.15
N	6659	8070	8295	6732
"LL"	4200.12	5141.16	4220.34	3610.22
BIC	8409.05	10291.32	8449.7	7229.25

Note: *p < .10, **p < .05, ***p < .01.

The country-level results are also telling. It appears that there is a significantly stronger support for state ownership in the Russian Federation as opposed to Ukraine and Belarus, while the support for democracy is significantly lower. These results point to interesting country-specific differences, which warrant further investigation.

As we expected, the personal values have a significant effect on the citizen's attitudes toward the state and economy. The collectivist values are positively and highly related to the support for the strong role of the state and negatively related to the attitudes toward income inequality. Conversely, the humanistic values also have a negative effect on the attitudes of the strong state. The individualistic values also have a negative effect on the role of the strong state. Yet, most importantly, the individualist values have a large positive effect on favorable view of democracy as a preferable form of government.

The temporal fluctuations in attitudinal trends among the four generations represent the effects of conditions to which individuals were exposed during these time periods. As we hypothesized, the fourth generation is most profoundly impacted by the transition. As a result of the experience with the economic hardship of the transitional decades, there is a general increase in the support for state control of ownership among all four generations. However, the fourth generation remains most disapproving of state ownership, suggesting that the fourth generation has been most impressionable during the transitional decade of the 1990s.

The transitional effect on attitudinal change is also vivid when it comes to generational views of income inequality. Again, there is an overall decline in the support for income inequality among the first three generations. Yet, we see that the fourth generation was the least supportive of income inequality in the early days of transition. This trend supports our previous findings about the effect of economic transition on the fourth generation.

The empirical results presented in Tables 1.3 and 1.4 provide us with evidence to support our expectations about the nature of intergenerational differences between the transitional generation born between 1973 and 1983 and the previous generations of Soviet citizens. The results suggest that the fourth generation is more supportive of individualist values, democracy, and market economy than the previous three generations. Moreover, the odds ratios point out the distance in attitudes that set the fourth generation further apart, supporting our claim that the experience of the socioeconomic transition during the developmental socialization period had profound effects on the members of this generation.

We now turn to the qualitative analysis of the in-depth interview in order to highlight the transitional experiences and the effect they had on the attitudes of the respondents.

EVALUATION

Generations are not formed in a vacuum, and their formation depends on the social, historical, political, and economic contexts in which they emerge and operate. This part of the study investigates cultural, historical, geopolitical, and economic factors that account for the differences in the norms, beliefs, and perceptions of the Soviet generations and the generation of the 1990s. This part is based on the 20 in-depth interviews with Russians, Belarusians, and Ukrainians who were born in the 1980s and whose teenage years were in the 1990s (Appendix B offers descriptive statistics on the interviewees). The purpose of the interviews was to provide an in-depth understanding of the intracountry events and processes and also substantive cross-country comparison of personal experiences. This explains peculiarities of the formation and establishment of the new regime and also the mechanisms through which the transition from one system to the other influenced the formation of norms, ideas, and beliefs of the new generation.

The interviews gave access to greater levels of information and a more complete picture of the intracountry and intercountry contexts and case-specific insights and resulted in a rich set of qualitative data. It is important to note, however, that the interviews go beyond mere description as they were conducted with the aim of contributing to testing the hypothesis about the existence of the generational gap between the norms, values, and perceptions of the Soviet generations and the generation of the 1990s, and also the influence of the new social, political, and economic realities on norms and values of the new generation. A diverse range of respondents enhanced the credibility of the answers, and an in-depth interview format allowed for follow-up questions and ensured consistency across the answers provided.

The interviews support the findings of the quantitative analysis carried out in this chapter and confirm the existence of a significant generational gap. The factors that shaped and influenced the norms and values of the new generation can be divided into two broad interconnected categories: politico-economic and sociocultural.

Politico-Economic Factors

By introducing privatization and letting the market rather than the government determine prices and output levels, the reformers hoped to create an incentive structure in the economy and encourage competition, risk, independence, and efficiency. The general assumption was that only by destroying everything that was in the old system could the centrally planned economy be dismantled and a new well-functioning capitalist system be created. However, in practice, these drastic reforms had a detrimental effect on the society. Privatization reform radically concentrated wealth and power in the hands of a few, led to a severe stratification in society, and destroyed labor's bargaining power and social safety nets. At the same time, economic liberalization worsened already significant hyperinflation and led to the bankruptcy of much of the industry and economic activity in the countries of the former Soviet Union. Following the economic crisis of the early 1990s, post-Soviet states experienced not only a sharp increase in the rates of poverty, unemployment, and economic inequality, but also a dramatic decline in public health indicators, medical services, and life expectancy.

The aforementioned economic reforms of the 1990s led to those on fixed incomes (the majority of the population) suffering a severe drop in living standards, and having their lifetime savings wiped out. The purchasing power of the population was drastically reduced, so while the stores had abundant goods after the opening of the borders to imports, workers could now afford to buy very little, if anything, as there were constant delays of payments in almost every sector of the economy. One of the interviewees recalled:

> The most difficult thing was there was nothing to eat—literally nothing to eat. My parents worked at a big factory, and their wages were constantly delayed or not even paid at all. Then the factory closed and a series of useless shops were opened there. I had been so proud of my parents and the factory, and I did not understand why, instead of cool machines, someone installed meaningless shops with cheap Chinese products.

Another interviewee reflected on the transition years with a bit of humor:

> For me this time [of transition] is associated with hunger and queues. It is associated with noodles and cheese, the absence of all food products. For me that time is hungry and cold time. [… At the university] we were friends with the young men from Chukotka. They were studying on state scholarships, so then the "brains" could return back to Chukotka. Their parents would send them huge cans of red caviar. I remember this very well. They did not have enough money to buy even the Chinese noodles. They would cook a tiny amount of those noodles and then eat caviar with huge table spoons. You see, the caviar supply was abundant, but the noodles were in deficit.

It is now an accepted truism in the literature of postcommunist transition that the economic reforms created a sharp distinction between winners and losers in post-Soviet societies (Kitschelt, 1992, 1995). Some benefited from the competition and opening of the borders for the transfer of goods, capital, and labor; the majority of the population suffered. Among the obvious winners were a new class of entrepreneurs, black marketers, and racket gangs that had already emerged under Gorbachev's Perestroika reforms. Another particular type of winners were the former technocrats of the Communist Party, KGB, Komsomol, and other governmental organizations that managed to obtain enormous privileges in the new economy. Some secretly transferred the assets of their organizations to offshore investments and gained enormous profits in overseas markets. Others used their political connections to obtain access to Western lending and economic assistance programs and created banks and businesses, or used their insider positions to win lucrative government contracts at artificially low prices and financial credits at artificially low interest rates, or acquired overnight fortunes from the official privatization program. As one of the respondents recalled:

> Privatization and vouchers were the biggest scam. Whoever had political connections happened to be near "*kormushka*," or the trough—those people earned fortunes overnight. The rest were incredibly poor. A small group of people managed to either open or work for new businesses (like my parents), but it was definitely a minority and they were constantly subjected to economic terror from racketeers. Now it is all legalized-racketeers are government servants. They take enormous "otkati," bribes, in exchange for allowing businessmen to live in peace.

The delegitimization of the public sphere, degradation of state services, and "oligarchization" of the economy led to a widespread opinion that decent people should avoid politics. Therefore, younger people tried to find room for expression outside political realms and policy arenas.

At the same time, it is important to note that a few people, without particular political, social, or economic status but with a lot of entrepreneurial spirit, found significant opportunities in the economic legal and general confusion of the postcommunist transition and managed to accumulate considerable wealth from either general trade or domestic production. However, their position was quite shaky as they became the primary target for the black market racketeers and criminal groupings. For instance, one of our interviewees recalled the following:

> My friends and I were good in foreign languages and we opened a small private school in Samara to help kids with language exams or help high school students enter universities demanding good knowledge of foreign languages. Well, we were immediately approached by racketeers and had to pay them 20 percent of what we earned for "protection."

Another respondent recalled:

> Well, our republic [Chuvashiya] was very criminal, because we were close to Kazan. And Nizhny Novgorod, I think, was relatively quiet. But in our area

there were [criminal activities in the markets] you know, also there were these
criminal wars. ... And there was cruelty. And the young people were tough. I
remember, although it did not involve me, thank God, because we had healthy
relationships in our school environment, however, in general, around us, there
was a lot of aggression.

Another respondent recalled:

My father was blackmailed and had problems with criminal groups. My parents
had to pay a lot to settle the issue. And the whole family was scared that I could
be kidnapped (it was quite possible).

Thus the teenagers of the 1990s whose parents were among either the
old *nomenklatura* that cashed in on new opportunities or the new class of
entrepreneurs, or who joined such new entrepreneurial or criminal groupings, gained significant material benefits—though, of course, had very risky
lifestyles. Those young people who lived in regular families on incomes provided by the government budgets suffered immensely despite their parents'
high levels of education and advanced skills.

However, both winners and losers claim that with the destruction of stability and predictability that the societies enjoyed under the Soviet regime,
a new system of values and new features of character started to develop:
individualism, independence, self-reliance, persistence, resourcefulness, and
adventurism:

I think my generation was very influenced by the change in the system. During
the days of the Soviet Union, there was stability, but no personal liberty.
Government was the guarantee of everything and individual initiative did not
matter much. People knew that when they graduated from university they will
automatically have jobs provided by the government, etc. The level of job
security was very high. And then everything changed significantly. ... The
government collapsed and people had to rely only on themselves. That is, it was
an open market, free market. ... Of course, I (and my generation in general)
became very materialistic, money oriented, pragmatic, and tough. At the same
time, we are much more flexible, adaptive, and resourceful than our parents. ...
Also we wanted more freedom and democracy than our parents. I would say we
are absolutely not like our parents.

Another interesting aspect of the postcommunist transition is that even
those who suffered a lot due to severe economic decline, degradation of social
services and other negative effects of transition, perceive the transition period
in a romanticized limelight, as their teenage-hood and associated experiences
(first love, first job, relative independence, travel experience, etc.) occurred

during this period. Nearly all the interviewees claimed that the 1990s made their character stronger, though they became less optimistic of collective action and governmental support.

As an example, one of the interviewees recalls:

> Despite all the hardships, there was a general feeling of the wind of change and hope. There is some truth in collapse and chaos, because to create something new you sometimes need to destroy the old. My parents were very scared of this destruction and did not want any changes. But me and my friends had very passionate discussions of our future and were hungry for the new times. This anticipation and uncertainty was very precious to us. ... There were eight of us and we formed an informal cooperative: We were gathering metallic bottles and other metallic stuff, selling it, and saving for future "big business." By the way, one of us is now the director of recycling plant in St Petersburg. I think our generation is much more creative than the previous ones, because we do not have any ideological dogmatic frameworks imposed on us, and when we were growing up, a lot of things became allowed that our parents could not even think of.

Sociocultural Factors

The opening of the borders led to an intensified exchange of opinions, ideas, norms, and practices between the East and the West. Migration, markets, and social networking led to increased interaction, interconnectedness, and interdependence, creating a high level of human interpenetration. Through various exchange programs, cross-border economic and political activities, and tourism, broader publics were exposed to diverse opinions and mediums through which to interpret postsocialist life.

One of the respondents recalls this from his first trip abroad:

> I was shocked and impressed how big, colorful, and different the world was and was sorry for my parents that they did not have a chance to travel outside the Soviet bloc. I think people should be exposed to diversity and have chances to visit different places, to interact with other societies to get new ideas. Traveling developed my curiosity, open-mindedness, and tolerance.

At the same time, in the countries of the former Soviet Union, the disintegration of the central system that imposed a central Soviet identity produced its own important consequences. The collapse introduced the questioning of personal identities and belonging. As one of the respondents recalled:

> I realized that I was a Tatar and it was different from Russian. Before that, I knew we had relatives in Tatarstan and I liked to visit them with my parents, but I was not ethnically different in my class from other boys. With the fall of

the Soviet Union for some reason it became very obvious and I had difficulties
in school, because I was suddenly different.

Various interviewees claim that, ironically, communism was universal-
ist rather than ethnocentric and provided a general framework for broader
interethnic and supranational cooperation and communication. With the collapse of the Soviet regime, older ethnic and cultural tensions got activated
and became vibrant across the post-Soviet geographical continuum. At the
same time, the respondents claim that despite ethnic tensions and differences,
generations are similar and intergenerational differences persist across the
countries. Another respondent from Makhachkala, Russian Caucasus, recalls:

> Even though Dagestan was not as separatist as Chechnya, there were still strong
> discussions of our difference from the central Russia. Nevertheless, I think that
> Dagestani people of my generation have a lot in common with any other Rus-
> sian of the same generation since we lived through the same socioeconomic
> and political transformations. We also have similar sociocultural orienteers.
> For example, we all listened to Nautilus (popular music band of the 1990s),
> read Dovlatov and Solzhenitsin. I think we have similar characters: much more
> independent, proactive and flexible that those of our parents.

At the same time, all the interviewees point at a significant Western influence
on the values and tastes of post-Soviet generation:

> Western culture, music, tastes, fashion, and beliefs in a rational, atomistic, and
> progress-oriented society changed many of our traditional cultural values dur-
> ing the 1990s. We all wanted a VHS player, everyone wanted one. If someone
> did not have one, then they all got together to watch a movie. Everyone else
> watched, so we had to too; not necessarily because of the quality, but because
> it was so mainstream at the time. We all wanted to see how people live abroad,
> what their interests and values are. My parents used to joke that Beatles and
> jeans destroyed Soviet Union. Well, my generation was definitely obsessed with
> Western music and videos. We all wanted to imitate western lifestyle, to become
> more individualistic, creative and self-reliant.

On the other hand, an opportunity to compare and evaluate your own
culture through this comparative perspective enabled Russian, Ukrainian,
and Byelorussian populations to slowly awaken and recognize their ancient
past, which created interest in history and spiritual development. The interviewees argue that these processes gave rise to many trends that became
widespread in 2000s, such as an interest in Christianity and at the same time
old pre-Christian traditions: development of folk music, development of historical reconstruction societies, etc. These tendencies became interestingly

interwoven in a rough capitalist framework and increase in materialistic values and orientations.

CONCLUSION

The goal of this chapter was to highlight the last generation of Soviet citizens, whose socialization period coincided with the liberalization years of Gorbachev and with the political and economic transition following the collapse of the Soviet Union, as a generation that stands apart from Soviet citizens of earlier generations. The postcommunist transition was a phenomenal and tremendously difficult process that resulted in a large displacement of social, economic, and political orientations and also in major changes in values and perceptions among the last generation of Soviet citizens born in the last two decades of the Soviet Union. This new generation, which simultaneously experienced the socialization into the withering, albeit institutionalized, socialist state, the liberalization of the last decade, and the postcommunist transition, became very different from the previous generations that were raised during the Soviet times. Our findings, therefore, suggest that contrary to the expectation of accepted sociological theories, people of different generations who are socialized under the same sociopolitical system have more in common with each other than people who are socialized during the period of politico-economic transition and people of the preceding generation. The highlight of this "generational gap" is the main contribution and novelty of this study.

With the use of quantitative large-N and qualitative interview analysis, we hoped to show that the post-Soviet transition gave rise to many individualistic and adventurist features that were completely nontypical of collective Soviet society. It increased the level of self-consciousness, self-reliance, and independence in a younger generation. At the same time, the transition period of the early 1990s created a certain fascination and admiration of Western-type lifestyle and the system of values. Harsh economic conditions, social and political degradation, and new realities enabled young people to mature very fast and evaluate their lives and the experiences of their parents and those of their own through the prism of the major transition of the politico-economic system, which was not only about politics and economics, but also, largely, about the way of thinking and perceiving life. The data presented by the interviews highlight these developments.

The analysis presented in this chapter clearly shows the presence of a large generational gap, which we believe was a result of the transition itself. Building on the theoretical foundation of "generational conflict" developed by Mannheim (1952) and developed by a series of sociologists (Alwin &

McCammon, 2003; Dunham, 1998; Edmunds & Turner, 2002), we sought to show that the generation whose socialization period coincided with the postcommunist transition developed a set of values very different from their parents and grandparents. The result of the logistic regression employed here also highlights that the so-called generational gap is much larger between the transitional generation and their older counterparts. The effects of this phenomenon will have long-term repercussions in the post-Soviet space, and will be revealed in future policies and national politico-economic and geopolitical strategies.

While this chapter focused on three Eastern European postcommunist countries, Belarus, Russian Federation, and Ukraine, we believe that our findings are applicable to the generational difference in the entire postcommunist region. Many agree that the politico-economic transformation of the 1990s produced similar macroeconomic effects on all the regions and ethnicities of the Soviet Union. As such, we chose to focus on the level of the citizens as a whole. However, as our results indicate, certain cross-regional variations between the vast geography of the former Soviet Union exist. These cross-regional variations could arise due to ethno-national experiences. Chapter 2 turns to these cross-regional variations.

NOTE

1. The politico-economic transformation of the 1990s produced similar macroeconomic effects on all the regions and ethnicities of the Soviet Union; therefore, we choose to focus on the level of the citizens as a whole. While we expect that there might be certain cross-regional variations that could arise due to ethno-national compositions and appreciate the value of the research into ethno-national variation, such meso-level analysis is not a goal of this particular work of research.

Chapter 2

Generational Differences in Values in Europe

While the transition from communism proved to be a very significant event in the modern history of all postcommunist states, for some Eastern European countries, the transition was especially significant as it incorporated the process of accession to the European Union. The EU accession played an important role in enhancing institutional and market reforms in these countries. In order to comply with EU regulations, the economic, legal, and social structures of these countries had to be reformed and, as many scholars argue, the accession process had a profound impact on the new East European accession states in its own right (Schimmelfennig and Sedelmeier, 2005). The effects of EU accession on the internal structural transformation of the economy and polity of the acceding countries have been researched extensively (Featherstone and Radaelli, 2002; Schimmelfennig and Sedelmeier, 2005; Grabbe, 2006; Ekiert, Kubik, and Vachudova, 2007). However, there is another important aspect of regime transition: the change in the system of values, norms, beliefs, and perceptions of individuals.

The literature has addressed the cross-country differences and similarities in values in Europe. However, such analyses have been static and the dynamic analysis of the changes in value systems under the influence of macrolevel economic and political transition processes has been quite limited. This chapter conducts a dynamic analysis of the intergenerational and cross-generational divergences in values in the Central Eastern European postcommunist societies by focusing on the effects of postcommunist transition and European integration on value change across generations and by comparing the effects on the countries that became part of the European Union, their non-EU neighbors, and countries with EU membership prospects. The analysis presented in the following pages seeks to contribute to the burgeoning literature focusing on the normative changes in East Europe (Olson, 2002; Grabbe, 2002; O'Dwyer, 2006) by adding a unique intergenerational focus.

The existing literature on social change suggests that changes in values and attitudes can be attributed to two mechanisms: cohort replacement and intra-cohort change (Voicu, 2010; Firebaugh, 1997). The first mechanism relies on the assumption that values and attitudes are formed during the socialization period and remain stable as a person ages (Mannhaim, 1952; Danigelis, Hardy, and Cutler, 2007). The second mechanism suggests that values are influenced by life-cycle changes and therefore can change as a person ages and experiences life. Thus, according to the cohort-replacement approach, the intergenerational divergences are inevitable, variable, and most importantly stable, depending on the context that shaped the values of different generations. The intra-cohort mechanism, on the other hand, suggests that a truly profound sociopolitical event will influence all generations, thus intergenerational convergences of values are more likely. In this chapter, we take these theories of intergenerational difference as our starting point and analyze the effects of postcommunist transition and European integration on value systems of postcommunist Europe.

The chapter is organized in the following way. The first section positions our analysis within the larger debate on the effects of European membership on Eastern Europe and the concept of Europeanization as connected to the discussion of domestic normative attitude change. The next sections sketch the process of intergenerational value change and position it within the broader literature on value system shifts. Here we present our theoretical expectations and state our hypothesis. The Data and Methodology section discusses the data used in our analysis and the operationalization of our main variables, and spells out the logic behind the use of our statistical models. The following sections present the statistical analyses and provide the discussion of findings. The last section concludes with evaluation of our findings and suggestions for future research.

EUROPEANIZATION AND "EASTERN" ENLARGEMENT

There is no question that the European accession has produced profound impacts on postcommunist Europe. The research focusing on the accession and its effects on the Central and Eastern European states highlights numerous areas of domestic politics, economics, and society where European Union's influence are highly visible and tangible (Schimmelfennig, 2001, Sedelmeier, 2001, Sjursen, 2001; Grabbe, 2002; Bafoil, 2009). For instance, the development of functioning market economies presented a serious challenge for postcommunist societies. Given that these new states had very little if any experience with a market economy, the European Union has been instrumental in fostering the transformation (Iankova, 2002; Bafoil, 2009). Furthermore, the conditionality of accession directly influenced the flow and content of domestic public policy shaping the institutional and legal structures of the candidate states (Cerami, 2006; Cafaggi et al., 2010). The conditionality of accession has also brought changes into the social policies of Eastern European states. Inclusion of minorities, legal protection of human rights and environmental awareness were the main areas of focus (Cerami, 2005; Krizsan and Popa, 2010). Given the legacy of previous nondemocratic regimes and the multiethnic character of these societies, these policy changes also sought to foster tolerance, which is considered to be pivotal for functioning democracies (Di Quirico, 2005).

In light of the overwhelming influences of the accession process, some authors have suggested that accession proved to be one of the most important catalysts for successful democratization and socioeconomic development in Central and Eastern European societies (Schimmelfennig and Sedelmeier, 2005; Ekiert, Kubik, and Vachudova, 2007). Thus, we agree with previous research suggesting that accession has also functioned as a vehicle for disseminating ideas and transferring norms (O'Dwyer, 2006; Vachudova, 2007). Even though some studies suggested that the European Union created some political cleavages and contestations in East European Countries (e.g., Marks and Hooghe, 2016), the majority of the scholars claim that these cleavages can usually be related to specific topics (e.g., immigration) and they can be considered to be part of the democratic process; at the same time, the overwhelming majority of East Europeans whose countries joined the European Union or acquired "candidate" status became supportive of the basic elements and principles of democracy and free market.

One of the useful concepts that can help us tackle the value changes in Eastern Europe is Europeanization. As Olson (2002) points out, the word *Europe* has taken on an important political implication. Europe is no longer perceived as a mere geographic entity. It refers to certain set of institutions, policies, and values. In the literature, the concept of Europeanization has been used to discuss the effect of the EU membership or prospective membership on the domestic politics and society of European states. Although widely used, Europeanization is a very ambiguous concept and, as many scholars point out, there is no real agreement on its precise meaning (Borzel, 1999, 2001; Bulmern and Birch, 2001; Radaelli, 2000; Firestone and Radaelli, 2002).

Nevertheless, as Olson (2002) argues, although the definition of Europeanization seems to depend on a specific subject under discussion, it is a useful concept. Radaelli (2000) suggests that Europeanization implies dynamic exchange between domestic and EU-level institutions, practices, and values.

Furthermore, Radaelli (2000) suggests that Europe can affect more than "formal structures" of member states, "it can also influence the values, norms and discourses prevalent in member states." In his evaluation of the effect Europeanization on domestic structures, Olson (2002) proposes the following process of institutional and value changes:

> First, are changes in political organization: the development of an organizational and financial capacity for common action and governance through processes of reorganization and redirecting of resources. Second, are *changes in structures of meaning and peoples' minds*. That is, focus is on the development and redefinition of political ideas—common visions and purposes, codes of meaning, causal beliefs and worldviews—that give direction and meaning to common capabilities and capacities.

This observation suggests that the Europeanization of institutions and policy adoption create a favorable environment for the Europeanization of norms and values. As such, we should expect that value changes in the new member states will follow the political and economic changes associated with the enlargement process. For Eastern European states, joining the European Union quite literally meant adopting European institutions, policies, *and values*. The lack of a developed market, the lack of economic and democratic traditions, and certain cultural characteristics developed under communist regimes in these postcommunist states signaled potential problems and put into question the "European-*ness*" of these prospective members. Thus, Europeanization has taken on an added importance as a transformative democratizing force when applied to new Eastern European members and other potential postcommunist members (Featherstone and Radaelli, 2002). The Copenhagen criteria developed directly as a result of the "Eastern" enlargement illuminates the European Union's concerns about the lack of institutional capacity, democratic development, and free market in these prospective member states. Thus, the European Union's postcommunist member states have been undergoing the process of Europeanization alongside or as part of the postcommunist transition during accession to the European Union.

GENERATIONAL PERSPECTIVE

Sociologists have long argued that there are notable differences in norms and values from one generation to the next that contribute to the so-called "generational conflict" (Mannheim, 1952; Dunham, 1998; Turner and Edmunds, 2002; Alwin and McCammon, 2003). These differences occur because people who are born and mature around the same time experience historical events at the same time in their lives. These experiences, particularly during the formative years, can play an important role in shaping a particular generation. Firebaugh (1997) and Halman and Voicu (2010) identify this mechanism of social values change as cohort replacement.

Other things being equal, it is normally expected that the difference between two generations close to one another in temporal terms is smaller than the difference between generations further apart (Mannheim, 1952). However, we argue that the postcommunist transition is a major historical event that fundamentally altered the society and states at large and served as a generation-forming event. Therefore, as we shown in chapter 1 the generation whose formative years coincide with the transition is markedly different from other generations raised in the same political and socioeconomic regime.

At the same time, we suggest that Europeanization served as a consolidating mechanism and significantly softened the transition process in Central and Eastern European states that became part of the European Union. Thus, we expect smaller intergenerational differences in values in these countries than in their postcommunist non-EU neighbors, as well as significant differences in values held by corresponding generations in these two groups of countries. Moreover, we expect that the Europeanization process has led to a convergence of values between the generations of new member states and the corresponding generations in the "old" EU-15.

We expect to find sharp differences in these values between the younger and older generations in European postcommunist countries due to the dramatic effects of the postcommunist transition, which when coupled with the turbulent years of adolescence must have produced lasting effects on the younger generations, setting them apart from earlier generations raised in the same sociopolitical system. At the same time, as mentioned earlier we expect smaller intergenerational differences in countries that joined the European Union and therefore obtained a consolidating mechanism and a policy-learning model that made the transition smoother and provided appropriate guidance. We also hypothesize that there are significant differences in values held by corresponding generations in these two groups of countries and, over time, Europeanization and European integration lead to a convergence of politico-economic values between Western European and former communist countries in Eastern Europe that joined the European Union.

DATA AND METHODS

The analysis presented in this chapter includes two interrelated tracks of analysis. First, a logistic regression analysis and Pearson's correlations are applied to the World Values Survey data to analyze generational trends in politico-economic values.[1] These analyses illustrate the differences in politico-economic values between generations in the three groups of countries in Central and Eastern Europe—non-EU countries (countries that do not have EU membership perspective, at least in the foreseeable future), EU countries (Eastern European countries that became part of the European Union by 2008 (the last wave of the data available)), and countries with EU membership perspective—and also compare generational attitudes in these countries to those in Western Europe.[2]

Second, an econometric approach to country level panel data is used to examine the factors that explain the general change in values in Europe, with EU accession and Europeanization being one of the factors. A combination of these analyses allowed us to obtain rigor in the analysis of the transitional effect on generational value differences in postcommunist societies.

Modeling Generations

In this chapter, we use the World Values Survey (WVS) data collected in Central and Eastern European countries and European countries from the former Soviet Union (19 countries).[3] Since the main focus of our analysis is the three groups of countries mentioned above, we develop our generational stratification based on these groups of countries and compare these generations to corresponding generations in Western Europe. The four generations are modeled on the principles outlined in our introductory chapter.

BETWEEN AND WITHIN COUNTRY VARIATIONS

In this analysis, we use the WVS data from 2005 to 2008 to examine the true intergenerational differences in politico-economic values after postcommunist transition and Europeanization.

The goal of this statistical section is to show the differences in politico-economic attitudes (operationalized by the WVS questionnaire) among the four generations identified above and to compare these differences across the three groups of countries identified above.

To analyze the generational attitudinal differences, we use a logistic regression model. This model provides us with an estimate of the likelihood of identifying one or the other value or attitude as salient. We also use a method developed by Firebaugh (1997) to investigate whether the attitudinal variation is explained by cohort replacement or by intra-cohort changes. *Cohort replacement* explains (part of) the overall variation if younger birth cohorts are generally more supportive of the liberal politico-economic views than older birth cohorts. The underlying assumption is that values are socialized during childhood and early adulthood and are relatively resistant to change over the life-course (Inglehart, 1977). *Intra-cohort change* would

Table 2.1 Interest in Politics across Generations

	Non-EU Eastern countries	EU Eastern countries	Eastern countries with EU membership perspective
	Interested in Politics	Interested in Politics	Interested in Politics
	Coefficient/SE	Coefficient/SE	Coefficient/SE
Generation 1	0.268*** (0.007)	0.007*** (0.001)	0.014*** (0.001)
Generation 2	0.021*** (0.003)	0.175*** (0.019)	0.008*** (0.001)
Generation 3	-0.146*** (0.015)	0.103*** (0.011)	-0.099*** (0.002)
Generation 4	-0.308*** (0.013)	0.318*** (0.025)	-0.112*** (0.021)
Intra-cohort (%)	39.12	69.28	52.01
Cohort-replacement (%)	61.88	31.72	47.99
Education Level	0.622*** (0.034)	0.594*** (0.039)	0.604*** (0.026)
Number of observations	4,332	13,527	5,879
Chi²	1243	985	1734

Note: ***p < 0.01, **p < 0.05, *p < 0.1.

explain (part of) the overall change when members of some or all birth cohorts become more supportive of liberal politico-economic values over a given time span. This method allows for evaluating whether the variation in value orientation is coming from contextual changes that affect all the generations (intra-cohort effects) or from socialization of younger generations in a different cultural and sociopolitical context (cohort replacement). We assess intra-cohort and cohort replacement effects using the repeated cross-sectional WWS data in two steps. First, we estimate net intra-cohort and cohort-replacement effects by including survey year and cohort groups in a logistic regression analysis. Second, we apply linear decomposition approach and use the slopes for the year and cohort in the final regressions to calculate the relative importance of both sources of social change (Firebaugh, 1997). Education level is used as control in all of the models. Tables 2.1, 2.2a, and 2.2b demonstrate the results of the analysis.

First, we take a look at the overall attitude toward politics among generations (Table 2.1).

It is very interesting to note that among the four generations in non-EU countries, the transitional generation seems to be the least interested in politics. At the same time, in the countries of Eastern and Central Europe that joined the European Union, the fourth generation is the one that is the most interested in politics. As far as countries with EU membership prospects are concerned, the fourth generation is less interested in politics than other generations, but not to the extent as is the case in the non-EU countries. It is clear that although the generations in these countries are not as enthusiastic about politics as the countries that joined the European Union, intergenerational differences in attitudes toward politics are much less sharp than in the case of the countries without EU membership prospects.

In the context of post-Soviet states without EU membership prospects, this lack of interest in politics could stem from their experience with transitional politics and the absence of clear role models. During the difficult transition years when the situation on the ground did not seem to get any better regardless of what politicians did, the youngest generation might have learned that politics is not something that influences people's lives much. While politicians "play their games," it is up to individuals to fend for themselves. The Russian word *vertetsya* (to spin) defines a specific concept of the post-perestroika years and speaks clearly to this situation. One's own ability to "spin" and make ends meet is much more important than political deliberations.

At the same time, Central and Eastern European countries quickly oriented themselves toward integration into the European Union and thereby acquired a major policy-learning model. Therefore, their youngest generation was inspired by the prospect of joining the European Union and viewed the political arena as a feasible and legitimate means to promote their interests.

Table 2.2 Probability Analysis of Politico-Economic Values

	Non-EU Eastern European countries					EU Eastern European countries				
	Support for democracy	State ownership of business	Support for income inequality	Disapproval of economic competition	Support for state interference	Support for democracy	State ownership of business	Support for income inequality	Disapproval of economic competition	Support for state interference
	Coefficient/SE	Coefficient/SE	Coefficient/SE	Coefficient/SE	Coefficient/SE	Coefficient/SE	Coefficient/SE	Coefficient/SE	Coefficient/ SE	Coefficient/SE
Gener. 1	-0.326***	0.399***	-0.385***	0.178**	0.199***	0.006***	-0.067***	-0.057***	-0.084**	-0.191***
	(0.013)	(0.025)	(0.042)	(0.009)	(0.003)	(0.001)	(0.018)	(0.008)	(0.049)	(0.024)
Gener. 2	-0.073**	0.221***	-0.133**	0.053	0.105*	0.112*	-0.204***	0.093***	-0.104**	-0.134
	(0.022)	(0.008)	(0.049)	(0.061)	(0.052)	(0.069)	(0.009)	(0.015)	(0.053)	(0.150)
Gener. 3	-0.029***	-0.006***	-0.005***	-0.030**	0.012*	0.412***	-0.391***	0.118***	-0.428	-0.215***
	(0.002)	(0.001)	(0.001)	(0.015)	(0.006)	(0.008)	(0.025)	(0.014)	(0.514)	(0.013)
Gener. 4	0.118***	-0.311***	0.208***	-0.232***	-0.214***	0.316***	-0.301***	0.110***	-0.342***	0.027***
	(0.001)	(0.032)	(0.025)	(0.021)	(0.011)	(0.011)	(0.001)	(0.002)	(0.015)	(0.001)
Intra cohort (%)	28.84	35.53	38.09	41.45	49.47	51.04	72.83	66.62	64.89	77.03
Cohort-replacement (%)	72.16	64.47	61.91	58.55	50.53	48.96	27.17	33.38	35.11	22.97
Education	0.139***	-0.245***	0.286***	-0.322***	-0.344***	0.294***	-0.341***	0.299***	-0.406***	-0.285***
	(0.022)	(0.016)	(0.029)	(0.023)	(0.034)	(0.034)	(0.018)	(0.043)	(0.047)	(0.036)
N	4,332	4,332	4,332	4,332	4,332	13, 527	13, 527	13, 527	13, 527	13, 527
Chi²	1836	2574	935	1094	1845	1793	1004	1927	995	2008

Note: ***p < 0.01, **p < 0.05, *p < 0.1.

Various scholars argue that the youngest generation played a very important role in spreading European values in Central and Eastern Europe (Yenigun, 2008).

The next step of our analysis is to examine some of the more specific political and economic attitudes. Our focus here is issues related to the politico-economic regime and the role of state in the society.

The five regressions represented in Table 2.2 depict the generational attitudes toward democracy and the role of state in society and economy. Regression 1 illustrates support for democracy. Regression 2 presents generational attitudes toward state vs. private ownership of businesses and industry; the results show the likelihood of supporting state ownership. Regression 3 illustrates the support for income inequality. Regression 4 provides a glimpse into generational views on the value of competition in the economy. Regression 5 examines generational beliefs regarding state responsibility for ensuring that everyone in the society is provided for.

The differences between the attitudes of the four generations and intergenerational differences between the groups of countries are truly remarkable. In non-EU, European countries, the first two generations seem to be more likely to support a strong state presence in the economy and in regulating the well-being of citizens. On the other hand, the third and fourth generations (the fourth generation, in particular) are more skeptical of the role of the state in economic and social affairs and are in favor of economic deregulation and competition. Remarkably, however, the youngest transitional generation stands apart in its dislike for state regulation when it comes to income distribution. Individual responsibility to fend for oneself is more important than relying on external sources, particularly the government. Moreover, the government might be perceived by the new generation as a source of corruption during the postcommunist transition, rather than an equalizing source of social welfare it claimed to be during the years of the Soviet Union.

It is interesting that in non-EU European countries, general support for democracy is rather low for all generations. However, the fourth generation seems to be more in favor of democracy than other generations. This lack of general support for democracy can be explained by the immense disillusionment of people in former communist countries, where the transition to a market economy and democracy came with immense economic hardships, political instability, degradation of the education and health systems, and demographic and moral decline (Stiglitz, 2002).

In contrast to non-EU European countries, in Central and Eastern European EU member states, all generations, but especially the younger ones, are generally in favor of democracy. Additionally, unlike in non-EU countries, all the generations in postcommunist EU member states are in favor of economic competition and against state ownership of business. There also seems to be more appreciation of income inequality in Central and Eastern European EU members. As far as the countries with EU membership prospects are concerned, they show smaller intergenerational differences than the non-EU countries, but larger than the EU new members. In their value orientations, they are in between the non-EU states and the new EU members.

Figures 2.1–2.3 illustrate the intergenerational differences visually.

As is evident from these visual depictions the intergenerational differences are more pronounced and vividly spread out in the postcommunist non-EU countries. As Figures 2.1 and 2.3 show, the range of the generational differences on the issues of democracy and state interferences in the matters of economics are larger in the postcommunist non-EU states, at 0.4 to −0.4, than the range in the states with the prospect of EU membership, at 0.12 and −0.12. Moreover, the first glance at Figure 2.3 reveals that the generational variation in the postcommunist EU states, while present, lay on the same side of the 0 value. This suggests a general agreement and convergence between the folks of different generations on the general direction of the policy as well as the sociopolitical regime.

Substantively the figures reveal that on the issues of support for democracy and state ownership of business there is more intergenerational convergence and similarity between Eastern European EU states and those countries with membership perspective. There is greater divergence between generations on these important issues in postcommunist nonmember states.

The probability analysis revealed not only important differences between generations within the three groups of countries but also cross-generational differences between the three groups of countries. As far as the causal effects are concerned, it is also interesting that attitudinal differences in all the three groups of countries are shaped by both intra-cohort and cohort-replacement effects (as shown by percent of variance explained by these two types of effects in Tables 2.1, 2.2a, and 2.2b). However, cohort-replacement effect dominates in the case of countries without the EU membership prospects, intra-cohort effect dominates in the case of EU countries, and both types more or less equally explain attitudinal variances in the case of countries with EU membership prospects. This implies that political and socioeconomic contextual changes (like EU expansion) must have had a profound effect on shaping politico-economic values among all the generations of those countries that entered the European Union (intra-cohort effect), while differences in values in Eastern European countries without the EU membership prospect have been shaped predominantly by cohort-replacement effects: younger cohorts socialized in a different politico-economic context hold more liberal and modern politico-economic views and are, therefore, very different from their older counterparts. These findings explain the phenomenon of the generation gap that exists in postcommunist non-EU countries and much smoother

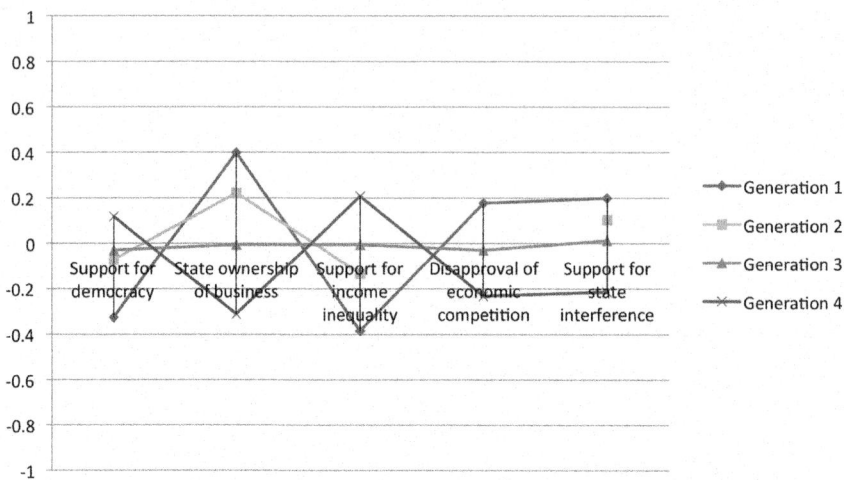

Figure 2.1   Non-EU Eastern European countries. Created by the authors.

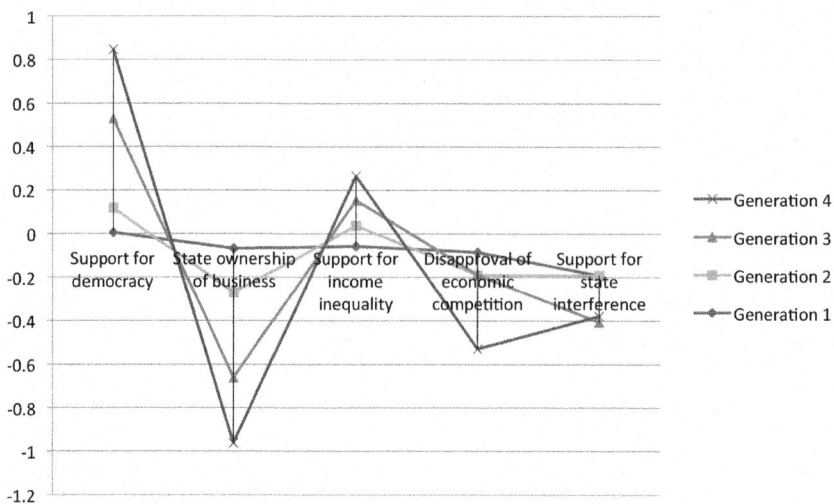

Figure 2.2   EU Eastern European countries. Created by the authors.

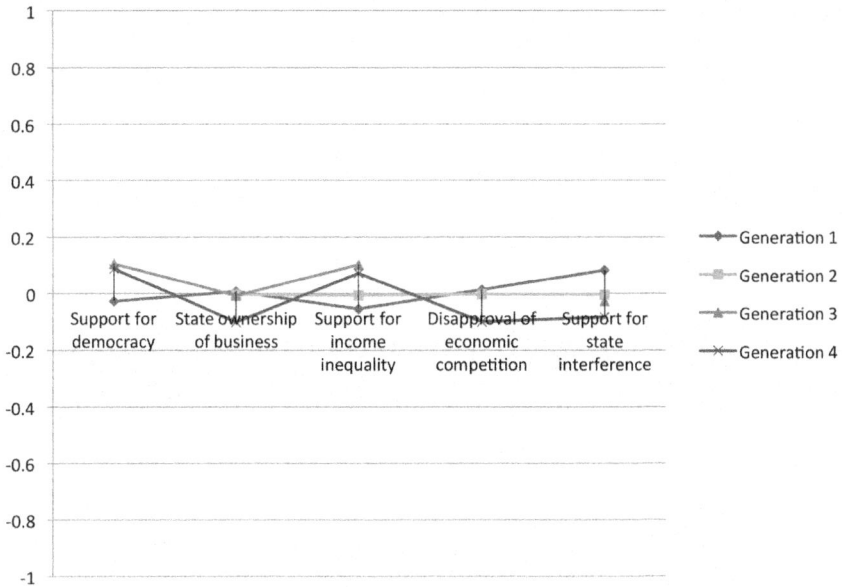

Figure 2.3   Eastern European countries with EU membership perspective. Created by the authors.

intergenerational differences in countries that became part of the European Union. It is also interesting that the countries with EU membership prospects stand in between being influenced by both contextual and cohort-replacement effect.

These findings are reinforced by our comparative analysis of the generational values of these three groups of countries with those of Western Europe. Tables 2.3 and 2.4 demonstrate Pearson's correlations in generational attitudes (the five politico-economic attitudes explored above taken altogether) between Central and Eastern European EU countries, Eastern European non-EU countries, countries with EU membership prospects, and Western Europe in 1990 and in 2005. We decided to take 2005 estimates instead of 2008 since a greater number of observations was available for 2005.

Correlation analysis indicates that in 1990 there was some convergence in the values of the first three generations both in and between the groups of non-EU members, future EU members, and countries with EU membership prospects. However, these generations had little in common with their counterparts in the "old" EU-15. This tells us that the experience with the communist system had a profound impact on generational attitudes among the adult population of Central and Eastern Europe. The fourth generation, however, exhibits different patterns. The transitional generation in future

Table 2.3 Probability Analysis of Politico-economic Values

	Eastern European countries with EU membership perspective				
	Support for democracy	State ownership of business	Support for income inequality	Disapproval of economic competition	Support for state interference
	Coefficient/SE	Coefficient/SE	Coefficient/SE	Coefficient/ SE	Coefficient/SE
Gener. 1	−0.027*	0.007*	−0.055***	0.014**	0.083***
	(0.006)	(0.003)	(0.004)	(0.007)	(0.004)
Gener. 2	0.009	−0.004***	−0.006***	−0.002*	−0.004**
	(0.012)	(0.001)	(0.003)	(0.001)	(0.002)
Gener. 3	0.106***	−0.008***	0.103***	−0.053	−0.027***
	(0.004)	(0.002)	(0.011)	(0.072)	(0.005)
Gener. 4	0.088***	−0.102***	0.072***	−0.100***	−0.084***
	(0.009)	(0.001)	(0.001)	(0.002)	(0.001)
Intra cohort (%)	51.93	52.04	54.09	56.85	50.22
Cohort-replacement (%)	48.17	47.96	46.91	43.15	49.78
Education	0.173***	−0.237***	0.239***	−0.428***	−0.358***
	(0.002)	(0.007)	(0.009)	(0.035)	(0.022)
N	5,879	5,879	5,879	5,879	5,879
Chi^2	0.0288	0.0316	0.0345	0.0382	0.0298

Note: ***$p < 0.01$, **$p < 0.05$, *$p < 0.1$.

Table 2.4 Pearson's Correlation of Generational Values: 1990

	1East_EU	2East_EU	3East_EU	4East_EU	1East_nonEU	2East_nonEU	3East_NonEU	4East_nonEU	1West_EU	2West_EU	3West_EU	4West_EU	1East_mem_per	2East_mem_per	3East_mem_per
1East_EU															
2East_EU	0.72***														
3East_EU	0.29*	0.49***													
4East_EU	-0.14*	-0.07**	-0.02**												
1East_non_EU	0.14***	0.31**	0.19	-0.52											
2East_non_EU	0.16**	0.11**	0.003*	-0.12*	0.82***										
3East_non_EU	-0.05	0.08***	0.04**	-0.33**	-0.13***	0.08									
4East_non_EU	-0.10*	-0.05*	-0.39	-0.23	-0.25***	-0.13**	0.12*								
1West_EU	-0.51**	-0.66	0.12	0.13*	-0.90*	-0.15	0.06	-0.19*							
2West_EU	-0.12*	-0.39***	0.14**	0.68	-0.88**	-0.34**	-0.22*	-0.15**	0.22*						
3West_EU	-0.50**	-0.09**	-0.06	0.11**	-0.56*	-0.17*	-0.07	0.03	0.12	0.28*					
4West_EU	-0.13***	-0.17	0.18	0.15**	-0.40**	-0.37*	-0.29	0.11	0.09	0.02*	0.23				
1East_m_per	0.49*	0.55***	0.04	-0.14	0.52***	0.42***	0.27*	-0.22	-0.63***	-0.50**	-0.31*	-0.29**			
2East_m_per	0.35***	0.21***	0.07	-0.09	0.26**	0.31**	0.12**	-0.14	-0.54***	-0.38**	-0.13	-0.24**	0.67*		
3East_m_per	0.20**	0.31*	0.13**	0.11	0.13*	0.10*	0.17**	-0.07	-0.27*	-0.16***	0.12	-0.18*	0.19*	0.12**	
4East_m_per	-0.06	-0.03	-0.02	0.19	-0.09	-0.07	-0.11	0.05*	0.04	0.02	0.07*	0.11	-0.08	-0.16	-0.26

Note: ***p < 0.01, **p < 0.05, *p < 0.1.

member states did not correlate with the transitional generation in non-EU members and countries with EU membership prospects. The fourth generation in the future member states experienced the "thaw" of the regime earlier than the corresponding generation in the former Soviet Union and the Balkans. The fourth generation in the future member states is the only one to correlate significantly with generations in the "old" EU-15 during the 1990s.

The correlation of 2005 values reveals some further interesting details and supports our expectation about value convergences. We can see more divergence between the generations of the new EU member states and the former USSR societies that did not join the European Union. One the other hand, there is generally more convergence between the new member states and the "old" EU-15. This suggests that the EU membership had a harmonizing effect on the value systems of these new member states. It is interesting that the countries with EU membership prospects show some slight convergence with the EU-15, but to a much lesser extent than the new EU members. At the same time, they do not show convergence with postcommunist non-EU countries, unlike in 1990. In order to visualize these trends, we include Figure 2.4, modeled in MATLAB software, which portrays cluster analysis of country value averages (without splitting the data into generations) fitted to the vector variable of "closeness to EU-15" values that consists of the politico-economic values that we explore above.

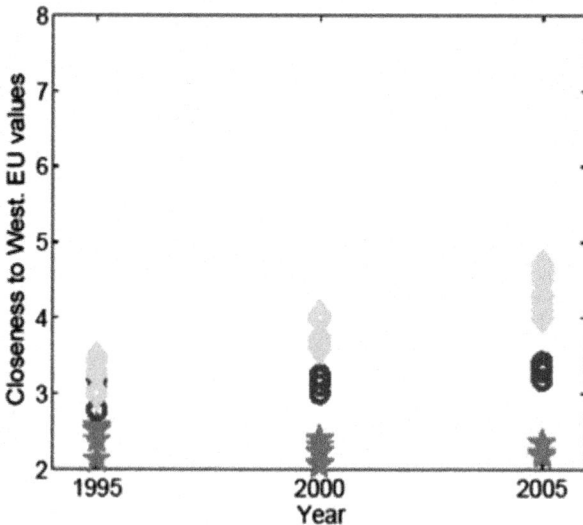

Figure 2.4 Closeness to the Western/EU Values among Post-Communist Eastern European Countries. Created by the authors.

The analysis indicates three distinct clusters: countries that were not "close" to EU values and that did not become closer overtime (these are non-EU countries); countries that were a little bit higher on "closeness to EU values" and that increased their closeness score significantly over time (EU recent members); and countries that increase their closeness scores, but very slowly (countries with EUmembership perspective). It is interesting that among EU entrants Czech Republic shows the fastest pace of value convergence over time, while Romania and Bulgaria are the slowest convergents. These findings have significant implication for the Europeanization literature as they show important harmonizing effect of EU enlargement on values in Central and Eastern Europe.

We now turn to a systematic empirical exploration of the effects of transition-related and EU-membership-related variables.

Factors of Change

To explain generational changes in values in Central and Eastern Europe over time, we use an econometric approach to panel data. This approach allows us to control for unobserved heterogeneity (or biases due to unmeasured differences among the units of observation).

Our sample consists of nineteen countries, each composed of four generations. The panel for the analysis is composed of four period observations for each generation (1990, 1995, 2000, and 2005). Therefore, there are 304 observations in the analysis. Our dependent variables are those explored above: generational attitudes toward democracy and state vs. private ownership of business and industry; attitudes toward income inequality, support for economic competition, and generational beliefs about the state's responsibility for ensuring that everyone in the society is provided for.

We explore a number of factors that can explain variance over time in generational attitudes between countries as well as a general change in values. Our main research variables are the effects of politico-economic transition (regime change) and Europeanization. Therefore, our independent variables are GDP per capita (World Bank data), Foreign Direct Investment (World Bank data), Gini coefficient (World Bank estimates), governance (World Bank data), EU assistance (financial assistance, EU Commission data), EU membership operationalized as a dummy variable, as well as EU membership perspective (dummy variable).[4]

We control for cultural factors, operationalized by Ingelhart and Welzel's scores on modernity (vs. traditionalism) and self-expression (vs. survival). Additionally, we include controls for the years under communist regime and the problem of stateness. The studies of regime change and democratic transition and consolidation suggest that the development of new regime-related attitudes can be influenced by experiences with the previous nondemocratic regime (Linz and Stepan, 1996). It is reasonable to expect that societies that spent more years under the communist regime are more deeply influenced by the doctrine and, therefore, their values will change at a slower pace. Thus, we include this measure as a control mechanism to account for earlier society-wide experiences with the depth and breadth of ideological state penetration. The problem of stateness has also been identified as a major obstacle in the democratization process and transition to a new economic system (Linz and Stepan, 1996). This problem occurs under conditions of hostility between ethno-national groups in a multinational state. Thus, this variable controls for the presence or absence of the intersocietal conflicts that might influence intergenerational value change during the transition. We also control for lagged value variables by imposing a 15-year lag to see if any predisposition toward more liberal politico-economic values might have affected change in values over time.

We estimate the following equation:

$$\text{Value } 1990\text{--}2005 = \alpha + \beta_1 X_1^t + \beta_2 X_2^t + \beta_3 X_3^t + \beta_4 X_4^t + \beta_5 X_5^t + \beta_6 X_6^t + \beta_7 X_7^t + \beta_8 X_8^t + \beta_9 X_9^t + \beta_{10} X_{10}^t + \beta_{11} X_{11}^t + \beta_{12} X_{12}^t + U_i + \varepsilon_{it}$$

Where the value for a given generation-year is a function of GDP per capita, Foreign Direct Investment, Gini coefficient, governance, EU assistance, EU membership, EU membership prospects, lagged-value, modernity, self-expression, years under communism and the stateness problem.

The error term in this equation is composed of two parts: a country-level effect that does not vary across time (U_i) and an idiosyncratic error term that varies across countries and across time points (ε_{it}).

Panel-data estimators help us avoid the shortcomings of traditional ordinary least squares (OLS) methods that ignore intra- or within-panel correlation. We use random effects model, which shows good model fit with our data and gives us a rigorous estimation of the model's parameters.[5] To account for the heteroskedasticity problem, we use robust standard errors. We also check for possible autocorrelation of idiosyncratic disturbances using the Wooldridge test (Wooldridge, 2002, pp. 282–283), the results of which indicate that there is no first order autocorrelation. Table 2.5 presents the results of the analysis conducted using the fixed effects vector decomposition model.

The analysis shows interesting results. Change in politico-economic indicators (i.e., politico-economic transition) and EU influences have strong significant effects on the change in politico-economic values. Therefore, support for a deregulated competitive economy is positively affected by effective governance, economic prosperity, EU financial assistance, EU membership,

Table 2.5 Pearson's Correlation of Generational Values: 2005

	1East EU	2East EU	3East EU	4East EU	1East nonEU	2East nonEU	3East non EU	4East nonEU	1West EU	2West EU	3West EU	4West EU	1East mem_per	2East mem_per	3East mem_per
1East_EU															
2East_EU	0.48***														
3East_EU	0.14***	0.15***													
4East_EU	-0.09**	-0.03	-0.09**												
1East_non_EU	0.02*	-0.27***	-0.33***	0.01											
2East_non_EU	-0.13*	-0.49*	-0.22	-0.02	0.92***										
3East_non_EU	-0.22**	-0.76	-0.11**	-0.18	0.05	-0.06**									
4East_non_EU	0.06	0.04*	0.07*	-0.16***	-0.29***	-0.20***	0.29								
1West_EU	0.002*	0.12*	0.29	-0.03	-0.15**	-0.39***	-0.07	0.25							
2West_EU	0.11***	0.27**	0.24**	-0.21	-0.34**	-0.15**	-0.08	-0.20	0.33**						
3West_EU	0.10***	0.07**	0.43***	0.17**	-0.47***	-0.91	-0.11	-0.13	0.17*	0.51**					
4West_EU	-0.24*	-0.05	0.21	0.62***	0.11*	0.03	-0.12	-0.17**	0.13	0.28	0.05*				
1East_m_per	0.26***	-0.02	-0.12	-0.03	-0.31	-0.05	-0.24	-0.67	-0.01	0.02	-0.09	-0.02			
2East_m_per	-0.15	0.17**	0.17*	0.07	-0.17**	-0.27	-0.12*	-0.72	0.03	0.12	0.17	0.07	0.06		
3East_m_per	0.18*	0.22	0.13**	0.20**	-0.17**	-0.11**	-0.04**	-0.19**	0.04	0.15	0.11**	0.09*	0.04	0.12*	
4East_m_per	0.16	0.17**	0.41	0.31***	-0.21***	-0.13	0.02	-0.08**	0.07	0.13	0.10*	0.14***	-0.01	0.14**	0.16**

Note: ***p < 0.01, **p < 0.05, *p < 0.1.

Table 2.6   Panel Data Analysis: Results of Analysis

	Support for democracy	State ownership of business and industry	Support for income inequality	Disapproval of economic competition	Support for state interference
GDP per capita	0.37***	−0.70***	0.51***	−0.52***	−0.57***
	(0.015)	(0.004)	(0.006)	(0.014)	(0.005)
FDI	0.28***	−0.66	0.69**	−0.14***	−0.34
	(0.049)	(0.728)	(0.232)	(0.032)	(0.421)
Gini	−0.02**	0.51***	−0.54***	0.006	0.03***
	(0.009)	(0.002)	(0.001)	(0.009)	(0.001)
Governance	0.10***	−0.19*	0.03*	−0.12	−0.15***
	(0.003)	(0.098)	(0.015)	(0.207)	(0.001)
EU assistance	0.08*	−0.42	0.70	−0.25	−0.13*
	(0.044)	(0.521)	(0.847)	(0.283)	(0.065)
EU membership	0.45***	−0.18***	0.17**	−0.48***	−0.21**
	(0.022)	(0.003)	(0.073)	(0.001)	(0.090)
Perspective of EU membership	0.01***	−0.06*	0.05	−0.18	−0.003***
	(0.001)	(0.060)	(0.071)	(0.245)	(0.001)
Modernity	0.66	−0.002	0.19**	−0.07	−0.13
	(0.762)	(0.043)	(0.093)	(0.086)	(0.246)
Self-expression	0.04**	−0.34***	0.49***	−0.09*	−0.52***
	(0.019)	(0.011)	(0.025)	(0.045)	(0.012)
Years under communism	−0.25***	0.33	−0.20***	0.30**	0.28***
	(0.001)	(0.448)	(0.002)	(0.144)	(0.008)
Stateness problem	−0.77	0.08*	−0.12	0.15	0.65***
	(0.885)	(0.039)	(0.169)	(0.162)	(0.001)
Lagged value variable	0.005*	0.14	0.22	0.0008*	0.09**
	(0.002)	(0.168)	(0.248)	(0.0004)	(0.039)
Overall R^2	63	44	59	41	47
N	304	304	304	304	304

Note: ***$p < 0.01$, **$p < 0.05$, *$p < 0.1$.

and, to a lesser extent (but still the effect is significant), by EU membership prospects. These finding have important implications for the research on EU enlargement and democratization in acceding and candidate countries.

At the same time, such variables as disapproval of economic competition and desirability for an increased state role in social, political, and economic affairs are negatively associated with the variables of economic growth, governance, EU membership, and EU financial assistance, and positively associated with income inequality (Table 2.5). Support for democracy has a reverse association with these variables (Table 2.5). Thus, in the European countries without any prospect of EU membership and considerable EU assistance and, therefore, any clear democratic and economic role models, the transition was especially harsh and created a significant gap between the older and younger generations. As demonstrated by the dominance of cohort-replacement mechanism in these countries, new generations that socialized in a different politico-economic context became very different from their older counterparts. As far as countries in Eastern Europe that joined the EU are concerned, the transition was considerably softened by EU assistance and the prospect of EU membership, which consolidated the society and alleviated some of the economic and governance problems associated with transition. Pressure from the EU led to the necessary reforms and the EU became the major policy-learning model for Central and Eastern European countries seeking EU membership. The dominance of intra-cohort effect in these countries speaks to the harmonizing power of Europeanization on all the generations and to Europeanization being the major vehicle of social change in these countries. Our findings indicate that the European Union played an important stabilizing role for values related to democratization and transition to free markets in these countries.

It is also important to note that the European Union has had some harmonizing power on the countries with the membership prospects that turned out to occupy an intermediate value cluster in our findings. Indeed, it has been argued in the literature—and this is supported by the available statistics—that countries with membership prospects receive significantly larger amounts of financial aid than the countries without membership prospects, which is captured in our "EU assistance" variable. Candidate and potential candidate statuses give the European Union an opportunity to effectively use its conditionality approach (Schimmelfennig and Sedelmeier, 2005).

It is also important to note that lagged values turned out to have a slight statistically significant effect on the following values: support for democracy, support for state interference, and disapproval of economic competition. These findings indicate that in countries where societal values already exist that support the transition reforms, the EU membership reinforces and deepens these preexisting values. In the case of non-EU postcommunist countries, the pre-existing values were—from the very beginning—less conducive to the type of reforms mandated by the European Union and so the "vicious" cycle of poor starting conditions, less EU involvement, and more turbulent transition results in deepening of the value divergences within these societies and between them and the EU-15.

CONCLUSION

The analysis conducted in this chapter indicates that the postcommunist transition was a very difficult process that instigated significant transformations in politico-economic value systems in Central and Eastern European countries. This transition was not merely about politics and economics but largely about attitudes, beliefs, and values.

Tremendous economic changes ranging from the transfer to a market economy to the integration of domestic economies into the common market system and new socio-political realities created considerable intergenerational frictions, especially in countries that did not join the European Union and which, therefore, lacked a strong consolidating mechanism to pull the society together. These societies also lacked good policy and economic models and considerable assistance and guidance in the establishment of the new regime.

In addition, our analysis demonstrates that over time Central and Eastern European countries that became EU members show a trend of convergence in politico-economic values with EU-15 countries. The European Union also appeared to show some harmonizing power on intergenerational frictions in the countries with EU membership prospects. Therefore, regional political and economic integration proves to be an effective instrument of common value creation. These findings have important implications for the literature on Europeanization and EU enlargement. Further research could use the upcoming waves of WWS and explore whether recent EU initiatives in the context of noncandidate countries such as European Neighborhood Policy, the Eastern Partnership, the Northern Dimension, etc. have a potential to influence societal values. For instance, our analysis shows the statistical significance of EU financial assistance variable, implying that increasing EU assistance for the neighborhood via a variety of the neighborhood programs can potentially influence attitudes in the Wider Europe. Further research could explore potential and the limits of EU's transformative power related to values through its recent external governance mechanisms.

As far as the new EU members and potential members are concerned, though politico-economic values are easier and faster to change than some of the cultural values, we can further expect that the spillover from convergence in politico-economic values will initiate change in more fundamental values. Chapter 3 explores the effects of soft power of the European Union on domestic value change in Ukraine.

NOTES

1. The World Values Survey is one of the most widely used quantitative databases in social sciences. While it is has been criticized for its Eurocentric and reductionist approach to values as well as inflexibility associated with all large-n datasets, this national level questioner taps into key dimensions of population's sociopolitical attitudes sought after by our inquiry. Moreover, the survey data allows for cross-national comparative research.

2. We use official EU sources to define "EU membership perspective" and we use the European Union's definition of candidates and potential members: http://ec.europa.eu/enlargement/countries/detailed-country-information/serbia/index_en.htm

3. Russia, Ukraine, Belarus, Moldova, Serbia, Bosnia, Albania, Georgia, Poland, Croatia, Hungary, Romania, Bulgaria, Czech Republic, Slovenia, Latvia, Lithuania, Estonia, Slovakia.

4. As mentioned earlier, we use official EU sources to define "membership prospects": http://ec.europa.eu/enlargement/countries/detailed-country-information/serbia/index_en.htm

5. To check for the adequacy of the random effects model vis-à-vis fixed effects, we conducted the Hausman specification test. The test indicated that random effects model is preferable with our data.

Chapter 3

Supranational Norms and Domestic Value Change

Evidence from Ukraine

In recent decades Ukraine has sought a closer relationship with the European Union. Moreover, it is believed that the begging of the recent Russia-Ukraine crisis originated when former president Yanukovych refused to sign a long awaited Associational Agreement with the European Union on November 21, 2013. That decision led to Euromaidan, the wave of popular protests at Kyiv's Independence Square. The brutal police tactics against the peaceful protesters only increased the public's disillusionment with the government. The unresponsiveness and cynicism of the presidential administration led to the so-called Revolution of Dignity, which deposed Yanukovych and resulted in the Russia—Ukraine conflict. Since the presidential election in May 2014, Ukraine has signed the Association Agreement and applied for the visa free travel program with Europe. A number of domestic reforms aimed at bringing Ukraine closer to the European Union have also followed in the last two years.

As we have shown in chapter 2, the process of European integration has undoubtedly altered the domestic policies of its member states. The increasing decision-making capacity of the European institutions throughout the years has resulted not only in member states adopting a wide range of common policies but also, arguably, a common set of norms. The influence of the supranational policies of the European Union on domestic policy-making is well documented in the literature (Goetz & Hix, 2001; Olson, 2002; Schimmelfennig, 2003; Schimmelfennig, Engert, & Knobel, 2006; Schimmelfennig & Sedelmeier, 2005). Recent studies suggest that the European Union has also ventured into a new field of highly contested cultural issues such as LGBT rights, which traditionally were deemed to be within the purview of national governments (Leconte, 2008). Through both horizontal (from the European Union to member states) and vertical (interactions between advocacy networks across member states) channels, Europeanization is affecting the political opportunity structures available to LGBT activists (Ayoub, 2013). While the formal ability of the European Union to implement common laws on LGBT rights is still limited, by facilitating such transnational advocacy networks and creating a common European narrative in support of LGBT rights, the European Union is effectively promoting a common norm in favor or LGBT rights across its member states.

However, a question still persists: Is the European Union capable of using this common norm to directly influence the attitudes of individual citizens on contested cultural issues, including LGBT rights? Studies so far examine the institutional and large-scale reach of Europeanization in the form of social movements, mobilization, and norm promotion through national elites. The change in domestic attitudes is usually attributed to the work of domestic activists and institutions. However, international organizations interested in facilitating positive change have been keen on promoting and funding such activities. This chapter explores the literature on LGBT rights and EU norm promotion and examines whether EU norm promotion has a direct effect on citizens' support for LGBT rights.

In this chapter, we use framing theory to see how Ukrainian citizens react to the European Union; more specifically, we ask how they react to a pro-LGBT rights message coming from a domestic source as opposed to EU sources. The fundamental question the chapter seeks to answer is—how powerful is the EU influence on the attitudes of non-EU citizens? Are supranational or national actors more effective in introducing change on highly contested and morally charged issues like the protection of LGBT rights?

A survey experiment conducted in spring of 2013 in Ukraine is employed in order to compare the ability of the European Union and the ability of domestic activists to influence citizens' attitudes on LGBT rights. Like most post-Soviet European countries, Ukraine presents a case of deep-seated homophobia. Moreover, at the time of our analysis it had no future prospects of membership and few formal ties to supranational organizations in Europe. Thus, it is unlikely that a certain "logic of consequences" (Wendt, 2001) would be operating among its public where some respondents with pro-EU views formally adopt EU-promoted views on contested matters in order to increase the country's chances of receiving EU support. With the European Union having even fewer channels of formal influence in Ukraine at present, it is particularly important to examine whether such "soft power" instruments as norm promotion can directly affect citizens' attitudes on contested issues.

THE EUROPEAN UNION AS AN ACTOR
IN LGBT NORM PROMOTION

The rights of sexual minorities are often seen as challenging the traditional morality of societies and therefore have historically been under the purview of domestic politics. In the last few years, however, the European Union has taken very determined steps toward regulation of these arenas. Since the adoption of the Treaty of Lisbon and with it the Charter of Fundamental Rights, the supranational institutions of the European Union have been venturing into areas traditionally outside their areas of competence.

As an economic union, the European Union's main concern has been workplace equality. The legal framework for addressing workplace discrimination on the basis of gender and/or sexual orientation has been rapidly developing in Europe. The Treaty on the Functioning of the European Union, the Maastricht Treaty, and the Treaty of Amsterdam laid out the provisions against discrimination on the basis of sexual orientation. The Charter of Fundamental Rights, fully legalized by the Treaty of Lisbon in 2009, makes the protection of the LGBT community applicable and binding on all member states. The Equal Treatment Directive assuring the equal treatment of gay citizens was also adopted by the member states. The European Court of Justice has made several rulings chastising the member states for their violations against homosexual citizens.

Despite these encouraging legal advances, formal protection of LGBT rights at the EU level is still in its early stages and less formal channels of norm promotion have been quite active. The European Parliament and, more specifically, the Intergroup on LGBT Rights has served as a watchdog and a forum for advancement of antidiscrimination policies and practices. Aside from direct advocacy from EU-affiliated institutions, however, EU norm promotion has arguably benefited the most from the mutually supportive relationship it has with transnational advocacy networks. Europeanization has provided ample opportunities for transnational LGBT activists to mobilize across borders and, when seeking domestic support, they have frequently framed the issue of LGBT rights as an "inevitable process associated with 'European' standards of acceptability" (Ayoub, 2013). When faced with a hostile national government, transnational activists can use EU actors and norms on LGBT rights as allies in their lobbying efforts. Moreover, charting a common European narrative that ties LGBT rights to the protection and promotion of general human rights is often seen to increase the persuasive power of LGBT arguments.

While the opportunities provided by the European Union affect mobilizational tactics at all levels of advocacy activism (Della Porta & Ciani, 2007), this is not to say that there isn't still substantial opposition to LGBT rights in all EU countries—opposition coming from both political elites and public opinion. Such opposition is particularly strong in the "newer" member states from Central and Eastern Europe, where the accession process, despite introducing several important changes into the domestic politics of these states in a very short time, has also created a perception of the European Union forcefully imposing its preferred liberal values, which in turn created a backlash against the European Union and the LGBT community (O'Dwyer, 2012). Moreover, there is still significant variation both among new and old member states in terms of strength of the LGBT advocacy movement and public support for the rights of sexual minorities. While the active involvement of the European Union and its LGBT narrative has been beneficial to the LGBT movement in some cases, it has also afforded opposition movements to frame the LGBT movement as sponsored by external forces who threaten national cultural values (Ayoub, 2014).

For nonmember states from the former Soviet Union like Ukraine this oppositional narrative is arguably more vocal and visible than the words of LGBT supporters. Prior to 2014, there were few formalized linkages between the European Union and Ukraine, and thus the effect of EU activism on public opinion toward LGBT rights would operate almost entirely through informal channels. Additionally, domestic and international activists were forced to operate in an environment of hostile governmental elites and conservative public opinion. The subject of homosexuality in Ukraine was a taboo during the Soviet era and remained as such during the years of democratic transition. While Ukraine decriminalized "consensual homosexual intercourse between adults" in early 1990s following the independence in 1991, sociological studies suggest that Ukrainian society remains largely homophobic (Martsenyuk, 2012). The nationalist project of nation building, after the collapse of the Soviet Union, depicted homosexuality as detrimental to the development and growth of the nation. Homosexuality is often thought of as morally reprehensible challenge to the traditional patriarchal family structure.

Additionally, despite what is often expected to be a linear trend of ever-increasing support for LGBT rights in most countries, the tolerance for homosexuals and other minorities decreased between 2002 and 2007 (Martsenyuk, 2012), although regional and demographic variation in support for LGBT rights exists. Western regions of Ukraine, where religiosity and church attendance are higher, show higher levels of intolerance for gay citizens and their rights.

The general perceptions of homosexuality as immoral, perverse, and unnatural are also shared by a multitude of Ukrainian politicians from all sides of the political spectrum. The policies of the state under Yanukovych reflect these beliefs. In January and February of 2013 the Yanukovych administration attempted to push several antigay laws with the help of a loyal majority in the national legislature. Mirroring Russian anti "gay propaganda" laws, Yanukovych's laws would have made illegal any media or publications "promoting" homosexuality. Both the European commission and the European Parliament (EP) responded with harsh criticism toward these efforts. The EP suggested that this legislative proposal would play a great role in European Union's decision about relaxing visa requirements. Thus, the voice of the

European Union in promoting liberal values in post-communist nonmember states can still be heard, albeit having to contend with much more vocal opposition. Any direct influence that EU LGBT frames may have on citizens' attitudes in Ukraine's deeply conservative society would be encouraging news not only for LGBT activists, but also for the European Union's "soft power" in the region since formal political channels would likely decline even further following Russia's involvement.

ELITE CUES AND LIBERAL NORM PROMOTION IN THE EU'S NEIGHBORHOOD

When promoting tolerance and support for the LGBT community, international and domestic activists are hoping for two key outcomes: first, influencing policy in their desired direction; and second, influencing public opinion. In a world of informational abundance and a multitude of dissonant voices on any given issue, it has been documented that citizens often take social and political cues from political elites they trust and, by extension, from the mass media (Zaller, 1992). Political communications scholars have long recognized the importance of source cues. In particular, Druckman (2001) finds that not all elites can manipulate public opinion with equal facility; rather, framing effects occur when "citizens delegate to *credible elites* for guidance" (1061, emphasis added). That is, citizens will only believe message frames that are delivered by a source they believe is both trustworthy and knowledgeable about which considerations are relevant to a decision (Lupia & McCubbins, 2000). Source credibility also plays a similar role in moderating the influence of direct persuasion (Petty & Wegener, 1998) and media priming (Miller & Krosnick, 2000). Hence, a reasonable proposition is that source credibility also moderates the messages received in support of gay rights. But in the rough-and-tumble world of real politics, what constitutes a credible source on contentious cultural issues such as the rights of sexual minorities?

The most immediate answer would be national actors such as government representatives and partisan leaders. The dominant model of mass opinion formation introduced by Zaller (1992) posits that most people's views are marked by ambivalence and, to a varying extent, can be affected by news reporting. Most empirical work since then has focused on examining the ability and mechanisms of national elites in guiding public opinion on a variety of issues (Baum, 2010; Berinsky, 2009; Berinsky & Druckman, 2007). When national elites are divided on an issue, the elite cue-taking model predicts increasing polarization among the electorate. However, when most national elites are in relative consensus on an issue, less discord is expected among the population. As explained above, political parties in Ukraine, much like in the rest of the former Soviet Union, are rarely coming out in support of progressive policies on matters of LGBT rights and are, in fact, often seeking to restrict or marginalize the rights of sexual minorities. Consistent with this consensus model, recent surveys do find that support for LGBT rights is rather low in Ukraine (Martsenyuk, 2012; Stern, 2012).

On the other hand, government institutions are also heavily mistrusted in Ukraine, as in much of the rest of the post-Soviet states. Communist legacies, poor economic performance, and high levels of corruption in the years following the collapse of the Soviet Union contribute to the low trust in domestic institutions (Mishler & Rose, 2001a, b, 2007; Rose & Mishler, 1998; Rose, Mishler, & Munro, 2006; Wallace & Latcheva, 2006). Thus, it is not a straightforward assumption that national political elites would be able to have a strong influence on opinion formation when it comes to morally contested issues. Unlike more complicated policy debates, the cultural and moral realm of opinion formation is also highly dependent on socialization patterns, observed behavior in a person's network of social circles, religious beliefs, and ingrained national customs. Thus, it is unsurprising that post-Soviet states have the least supportive publics as compared to the rest of Europe when it comes to the rights of sexual minorities. Decades of social exclusion of homosexuals under communism combined with cultural conservatism on the matter would result in a difficult environment for the promotion of culturally liberal norms regarding LGBT rights. It is both historical legacies and unsupportive political elites that make the former Soviet Union a very difficult test of norm promotion on the matter of cultural values.

Non-governmental domestic organizations in support of LGBT rights, of course, do exist in Ukraine much like in all countries in the region. However, we question their ability to influence opinion. First of all, the NGO sector is comparatively underdeveloped in post-communist societies (Hrycak, 2006; Martsenyuk, 2012; Stepanenko, 2006). Secondly, domestic NGOs by nature of having less policy influence gain less media attention and, thus, citizens are exposed to their messages on an infrequent basis. Mainstream news reports are dominated by voices coming from the centers of power, which are usually the government, political parties, and any major political opposition (Bennett, 1990; Bennett, Larence, & Livingston, 2007).

NGOs and nonparty-affiliated political activists are thus restricted in their scope of influence and have limited access to media resources. This leaves us to consider the importance of foreign voices. In today's increasingly interconnected media world, European citizens are often exposed to information from foreign media sources. In the former Soviet Union, it is often the European Union and its affiliated bodies that garner top priority among foreign voices and are able to have its messages relayed in the national media. National political elites can also use relevant publications in foreign media outlets as additional arsenal in their own political agendas. For example, antigay rights advocates often cite the meddling of Western actors such as the European Union in their national traditions and the imposition of gay "propaganda" on their societies (Stern, 2012).

Foreign sources have already been found able to influence public opinion on certain matters even among the advanced industrialized democracies (Hayes & Guardino, 2011; Rouigrok & Van Atteveldt, 2007), whose citizens generally trust national institutions at a rate much higher than in the former Soviet Union. In addition, the European Union is often part of an important identity cleavage among the population of post-communist countries. In Ukraine, the European Union is often seen as a symbol of a "return to Europe" after the fall of communism and thus juxtaposed to Russian actions in the region (Hansen, 2006; Kuzio, 2000, 2008; Munro, 2007; Samokhvalov, 2007).

Therefore, we argue that the European Union will be the only elite actor whose media messages would be able to influence public opinion on the contested cultural issue of rights of sexual minorities. Two causal processes could be at work to explain this causal relationship. First, a sense of identification with Europe and/or the European Union can drive a real value adjustment among publics who repeatedly witness EU international actors promoting LGBT rights. Or, despite Ukraine's lack of membership prospects, a more utilitarian consideration could still be occurring where people see their future prosperity and protection from Russia linked to Western Europe and would thus rather follow the expected rules of behavior from Western actors while not really believing in them in private. While it is undoubtedly important to know which one of these mechanisms is at work here, it is beyond the scope of the current chapter. As a first step, we seek to establish the presence or absence of an EU framing effect on support for LGBT rights in the former Soviet Union. Should this be a real value change in the long run or a utilitarian strategy, it would still have important implications for policy in the region.

Data and Methods

To carry out the empirical test of our hypothesis we conducted a survey experiment in Ukraine. The survey took place in the spring of 2013. Subjects were recruited from a representative sample of citizens over the age of 18. A total of 217 adults participated in the survey.[1]

The experiment consists of two parts. In the first part, respondents were asked about their attitudes toward LGBT rights among a number of other relevant control questions. Two measures capturing different dimension of LGBT rights support were used. The first question mirrors the approach of the European Values Survey and asks respondents' opinions about having homosexuals as neighbors. This measure captures tolerance of homosexuality on a more personal level. The second measure is policy-oriented and was constructed in response to levels of agreement with the statement "Homosexual men and women in Ukraine should have the same legal rights as heterosexual citizens." The two measures are then combined into an index of LGBT rights support that captures both general tolerance of homosexuality in respondents' life and their willingness to grant legal rights to homosexuals.

We used the survey to conduct a basic test of the European Union's direct influence on support for LGBT rights. In the middle of the survey, respondents were randomly assigned to one of three short text frames related to LGBT rights. The first frame described EU efforts at promoting LGBT rights in Europe and in Ukraine in particular. The text of the second frame described very similar efforts but from the standpoint of domestic NGOs as the promoters of LGBT rights. Finally, the text of the third frame served as a control treatment and did not refer to LGBT rights, nor the European Union, at all. A neutral news story related to Latin American politics was used. Full text of each frame is available in the appendix. Text frames were kept short to avoid common testing problems such as respondents skimming through the text material or skipping it altogether in an effort to complete the survey faster. The three texts were also designed to have very similar word count in order for high equivalence between frames to be achieved.

Following the frame exposure, the second part of the survey again recorded personal tolerance of homosexuality and support for LGBT rights in policy matters. Different questions were used to avoid repetition with pre-manipulation questions. Personal tolerance of homosexuality was recorded by asking about the extent to which homosexuality can be justified—another common tolerance measure from the EVS waves. Secondly, the policy-oriented question this time asked about respondents' views on allowing same-sex marriages in Ukraine. The two measures were again combined into an index of post-manipulation support for LGBT rights.

We acknowledge that testing effects are a possible pitfall given the short time period between pre-manipulation and post-manipulation questions. To minimize bias stemming from respondents' tendency to appear consistent with the answers they gave before viewing the text frame versus after, we presented the survey as consisting of two separate surveys. This strategy helps separate pre-test and post-test content in a credible manner and reduces the degree to which subjects might assume a relationship between the questions preceding and following the manipulation. This procedure is consistent with deceptive practices employed in social psychological studies of attitude change, such as through cognitive dissonance (Cooper, 2007), in which pre-test and post-test questions are often identical.

Additionally, we controlled for several possible moderating variables such as the extent of having a supranational identity. Supranational identification was measured by asking respondents whether they see themselves primarily as citizens of their nation, of Europe, or of the world. This provides us with three levels of supranational identity strength—low, moderate, and high. While this study is particularly interested in EU effects on domestic value change, supranational identity can often serve as proxy for more than just support for the European Union and represent a certain type of cosmopolitan world outlook which is more frequently associated with liberal values. Therefore, we believe supranational identity, whether it is conceptualized as support for the European Union or as a cosmopolitan value outlook, can have a strong moderating influence on the effect of media frames on support for LGBT rights.

Additionally, we control for respondents' religiosity, their trust in domestic political institutions, their trust in supranational institutions (the European Union and the United Nations), their self-reported knowledge of the European Union, their interest in politics, and their demographic characteristics. Exact wording of each question can be found in the appendix.

Results

Looking at some basic descriptive findings, Figures 3.1 and 3.2 plot average support for LGBT rights by strength of supranational identity (low, moderate, high). In both cases higher supranational identity is distinctly associated

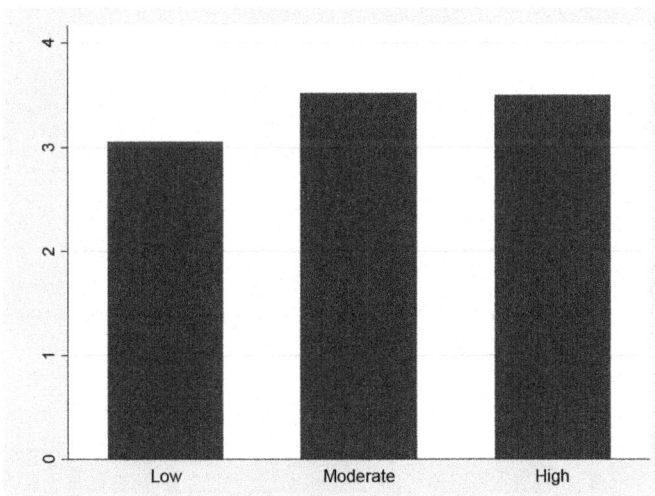

Figure 3.1   Pre-test Support for LGBT Rights by Levels of Supranational Identity (Low, Moderate, High). Created by the authors.

with greater support for LGBT rights, but the differences are strengthened after the frame manipulation. Figure 3.3 shows the effects of the three frames on respondents' post-test support for LGBT rights and, as expected, citizens exposed to the EU frame have higher levels of tolerance for homosexuality.

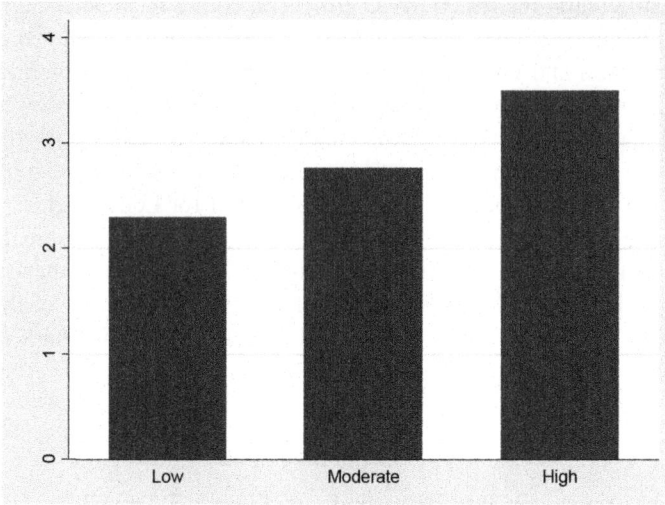

Figure 3.2   Post-test Support for LGBT Rights by Levels of Supranational Identity. Created by the authors.

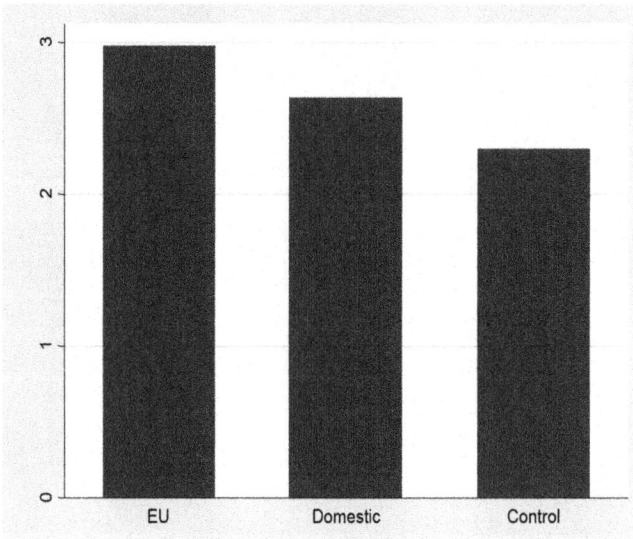

Figure 3.3   Post-test Support for LGBT Rights by Frame Type. Created by the authors.

Next, we test the effects of supranational identity in a series of multivariate models. The first column in Table 3.1 shows results from pre-test measures only. Even prior to any exposure to experimental manipulations, supranational identity has a significant positive effect on support for LGBT rights. Trust in supranational institutions also has a systematic relationship with the dependent variable, suggesting a consistent pattern of associating supranational bodies with more liberal views. From the remaining variables, frequency of church attendance has a strong negative effect on support for LGBT rights and women have a higher support than men.

The second column in Table 3.1 proceeds to show the effects of our text frames. Since respondents have already been exposed to the experimental manipulation at this point, additional dummy variables are included to

Table 3.1   Effect of EU and Domestic Framing on Support for LGBT Rights

	Model 1	Model 2
	Pre-test Support	*Post-test Support*
EU Frame	–	**0.547****
		−0.193
Domestic Frame	–	0.328
		−0.202
Religiosity	**−0.231*****	**−0.145****
	−0.063	−0.055
Trust in Domestic Institutions	−0.06	0.002
	−0.128	−0.113
Trust in Supranational Institutions	**0.298****	**0.157***
	−0.084	−0.073
Supranational ID	**0.277***	**0.497*****
	−0.126	(0. 114)
EU Knowledge	0.055	0.084
	−0.096	−0.091
Interest in Politics	−0.149	0.062
	−0.203	−0.177
Education	−0.037	0.093
	−0.108	−0.077
Sex	**0.607****	**0.612****
	−0.218	−0.181
Age	0.274	0.211
	−0.165	−0.152
Constant	1.43	−0.798
	−0.977	−0.708
R^2	0.163	0.252
Observations	191	191

Note: Entries are OLS regression coefficients with robust standard errors in parentheses.
*Statistical significance with 90% or greater confidence.
**Statistical significance with 95% or greater confidence.
***Statistical significance with 99% or greater confidence.

account for the type of frame the respondent read—one where LGBT rights were promoted by the European Union or one where domestic NGOs were the key actors. Results show that respondents exposed to the EU frame report systematically higher support for LGBT rights than those exposed to the control. Alternatively, the domestic frame does not produce statistically significant results. As theoretically expected, therefore, the direct influence of domestic political activists on public attitudes toward LGBT rights is over-shadowed by that of the European Union as a norm promoter. As with most framing studies, of course, we are aware of the possibly short-term effects of media framing on attitudes. However, even a short-term effect has an impor-tant implication since, given the presence of willingness and opportunity, it can be magnified through repeated exposure until it stops being a time-sensitive effect and starts to result in more permanent socialization.

Finding no effect of domestic norm promotion, on the other hand, is fairly understandable, given the facts outlined in the previous section of this chap-ter. With an underdeveloped NGO sector and low trust in domestic institu-tions, former Soviet Union states are rarely able to actively participate in and take advantage of the transnational activism networks developed within the European Union. Our data similarly shows that trust in national institutions is very low in Ukraine—more than 50% of respondents report they do not trust political parties "at all" (the lowest possible category of trust) while less than 5% indicate a level of trust at the high ends of the spectrum. Percent-ages are extremely similar for trust in the legal system while the government receives even lower degrees of trust. With respect to trusting supranational institutions, including the European Union, the pattern is almost the exact opposite, with approximately 51% of respondents clustering at the high end of the trust scale. In the case of the United Nations, for example, about 44% of respondents report high levels of trust.

Finally, Table 3.2 explores in a bit more detail the interaction between identity and frame exposure. The table presents conditional effects of supranational identity as moderated by the type of frame the individual has viewed. In the first column the EU frame is interacted with supranational identity, while in the second we examine whether the effect of supranational identity on support for LGBT rights is moderated by domestic norm promo-tion as well. Model 1 shows that exposure to EU-promoted calls for greater LGBT equality has a *galvanizing* effect on support for LGBT rights among respondents, with preexisting high levels of supranational identity. After viewing the EU frame, they exhibit greater support for LGBT rights. The magnitude of the effect is rivaled only by the effect of gender in our model. Additionally, supranational identity preserves its independent effect and is significantly correlated with the dependent variable even when an individual was not exposed to the EU frame. On the other hand, respondents with low

Table 3.2   **Moderating Effect of Supranational Identity on Media Frames**

	Model 1 EU Frame	Model 2 Domestic Frame
Supranational Identification	**0.313***	**0.540***
	(0.148)	(0. 130)
EU Frame	−0.430	−
	(0.416)	
Supranational Identification * EU Frame	**0.499***	−
	(0.232)	
Domestic Frame	−	0.381
		(0.494)
Supranational Identification *Domestic Frame	−	−0.204
		(0.301)
Religiosity	**−0.152***	**−0.166***
	(0.054)	(0.055)
Trust in Domestic Institutions	0.014	−0.015
	(0.115)	(0.119)
Trust in Supranational Institutions	**0.156***	**0.166***
	(0.072)	(0.074)
EU Knowledge	−0.087	0.101
	(0.092)	(0.092)
Interest in Politics	0.068	0.067
	(0.176)	(0.180)
Education	0.064	0.106
	(0.77)	(0.080)
Sex	**0.615***	**0.605***
	(0.179)	(0.181)
Age	0.228	0.199
	(0.156)	(0.158)
Constant	−0.166	−0.615
	(0.722)	(0.697)
R^2	0.260	0.223
Observations	191	191

Note: Entries are OLS regression coefficients with robust standard errors in parentheses.
*Statistical significance with 90% or greater confidence.
**Statistical significance with 95% or greater confidence.
***Statistical significance with 99% or greater confidence

levels of supranational identity who viewed the EU frame were not any more or less likely to support LGBT rights. Thus, EU activism does not yet have a *mobilizing* effect on our dependent variable—it operates best in conjunction with preexisting identification with a supranational body. Thus, while the European Union may be able to successfully influence public opinion on divisive cultural issues among its supporters, it is not capable of influencing its opponents on these contested matters. In essence, it operates similar to the way partisanship does in domestic political systems. Given the visible presence of an Europe/Russia cleavage in the societies of the former Soviet

Union, this result suggests that the there is still a notable opportunity for EU activism on LGBT matters in its neighborhood.

The second column in Table 3.2 presents a model examining whether the effect of identity on the dependent variable is also moderated by domestic frames. Findings indicate that this is not, in fact, the case. Individuals with higher supranational identity who viewed a call for LGBT equality disseminated by a domestic NGO were not necessarily any more likely to support the rights of sexual minorities. Domestic LGBT rights promotion did not have a mobilizing effect either—individuals with low levels of supranational identity and high levels of national identity were not significantly more likely to support or oppose LGBT rights after viewing the domestic frame. Overall, the findings in Table 3.2 strongly point to the conclusion that supranational identity has a moderating effect on citizens' reactions to LGBT frames. This effect can be galvanized by EU activism in the media. EU activism on its own, however, does not mobilize support for LGBT rights among those with lower levels of supranational identity. Domestic activism as portrayed in the media, on the other hand, does not seem to have a systematic effect on support for LGBT rights even among respondents with exclusive national identity.[2]

CONCLUSION

This chapter sought to examine the possible effects EU norm promotion might have on public attitudes toward LGBT rights in Ukraine, a non-EU-member state with very little formal experience with EU institutions.

The experiment revealed that higher levels of support for LGBT rights were prompted by EU framing while the domestic narrative had no systematic effect. This leads us to believe that supranational institutions face a significant opportunity to help shape attitudes on controversial issues in the EU neighborhood. However, our analysis further shows that supranational institutions reinforce or galvanize these attitudes primarily among persons who already possess higher levels of supranational identity. The scope of EU activism does not reach as far as mobilizing LGBT support among those persons who have low levels of supranational identification.

This kind of influence—though conditional on moderating factors such as supranational identity—is still greater than that of activism by domestic actors. Domestic media frames did not have the desired effect on soliciting support for the rights of sexual minorities. This is not a very promising development for the NGO sector in Ukraine—when the same words have greater credibility if uttered by international actors rather than domestic activists, the NGO sector is clearly in need of new strategies. However, some of that result is due to the extraneous political and economic environment and cannot be attributed entirely to NGO unreliability. Lack of funding coupled with hostility from the political elite to the LGBT cause and a conservative public create a most difficult scenario for the day-to-day operation of domestic LGBT advocacy networks.

For the purposes of this study the results presented in this chapter suggest that the European Union has direct and indirect effect on shaping domestic values in nonmember states. Yet, EU soft power seems to serve as a galvanizing effect among those citizens who already identify strongly with European values. As we have seen from the previous chapters this identity is strongest among the members of the generation "WhY." This seems to suggest that if Ukraine continues on the trajectory of closer relations with the European Union more shifts in domestic value system of Ukraine are possible.

NOTES

1. The survey was implemented by West Marketing Company whose services we hired for this project.

2. By "exclusive" national identity, we mean those who identify with a domestic entity (locality, region, or nation) as both their first and second choice of identification.

Chapter 4

Russia-Ukraine Conflict

Value-based and Generational Perspective

The recent Russia-Ukraine conflict unfolded in the aftermath of the Euromaidan Movement and the Ukrainian Revolution of Dignity when Ukraine's president Yanukovych fled Kyiv and the Parliament removed him from power the next day and appointed Turchynov as an interim president, who thereafter formed an interim government. While the new Ukrainian government was recognized by the United States and the European Union, it was rejected by Russia, which condemned the new government as the illegitimate result of a coup d'état.

At the end of February 2014, several demonstrations by pro-Russian and antigovernment groups took place in cities across the eastern and southern regions of Ukraine. Protests in the Crimean city of Sevastopol, seriously bolstered by the presents of unidentified armed men in military uniform without insignia (later revealed to be Russian), resulted in the Crimean Parliament voting to dismiss the Crimean government and a subsequent referendum on Crimea's autonomy. The ensuing surprising and highly controversial referendum on whether to join Russia had an affirmative vote, and while it was recognized by Russia, it was rejected by Ukraine, the United States, and the European Union, which described the event as a land grab by the Russian Federation and levied sanctions against Russia in response.

Protests in Donetsk and Luhansk regions escalated into an armed separatist insurgency with the Ukrainian government launching a military counteroffensive resulting in the ongoing War in Donbass region. Since the beginning of the insurgency Ukrainian government described the separatist forces as terrorist groups supported by Russia, which denies these claims. While two ceasefire agreements have been negotiated since the start of the conflict, the so-called Minsk I and II, they have not produced the desired results of ending the armed conflict.

While the conflict was unimaginable—even as the armed "green men" occupied Crimea in March 2014—for the many Russians and Ukrainians who believed in the fraternal relationship of these two nations, for others the conflict was an obvious and inevitable extension of what Anatol Lieven called "fraternal rivalry" (Lieven, 1999).

The purpose of this chapter is to shed light on the Russian-Ukrainian conflict by analyzing the dynamics of the Russia-Ukraine relationship through a constructivist approach to international relations by applying a value-based perspective. Thus, the focus of this chapter is a comparative analysis of the Russian and the Ukrainian systems of values, beliefs, and attitudes, ranging from values related to geopolitical issues to socioeconomic attitudes.

A value-based perspective is important in international relations studies and is useful in analyzing relationships between countries because it helps to better understand similarities and differences in the beliefs and motivations of people living in different countries. Peoples' beliefs and value structures play a crucial role in the collective identification process and form the core of a country's identity (Esses and Dovidio, 2001). At the same time, the construction of identity is also a political process (Arel, 2006); therefore, differences in views, beliefs, and value systems affect the relationships between states.

Following the generation focus of this book, this chapter analyzes the intergenerational differences and their role in the political processes of the two countries, as well as between the two countries.

The chapter is organized as follows. The following section presents a review of the literature that applies a constructivist approach to the analysis of international relations. It is then followed by the analysis section that is based on two-stage research methodology: statistical comparative analysis of Russian and Ukrainian value systems based on the data collected by the several waves of World Value Survey and then qualitative analysis based on the interviews, social media posts, and public statements of the officials and representatives of social and political movements. In the qualitative part of this chapter, we decided to focus on policymakers rather than common people to get deeper insights into the roots and the causes of the conflict. This focus also allows us to extract profound knowledge about the geopolitics and socioeconomic aspects of the conflict. The wealth of data availability, in part thanks to social media, allows us to focus on officials and the representatives of movements of both countries. The last section of the chapter concludes with prospects for future developments between the two countries.

THEORETICAL FRAMEWORK: INTERNATIONAL
RELATIONS AS SOCIAL CONSTRUCTION
OF MEANINGS AND STRUCTURES

According to constructivist critique, neorealist interpretation of international relations through anarchy and self-help, as well as, liberal interpretation based on the market forces and economic gains, are both lacking. These theories do not take into account important interests and identities of international actors. Constructivist researchers, on the other hand, argue that the analysis of values, beliefs, identities, and behavior of international actors should take a prominent place in theorizing about international relations (Brown, 2005). Constructivists profess that relationships between countries represent a kind of social interaction and exchange in coded frames based on the values and identities of the countries' populations (Checkel, 2004). Therefore, international relations are perceived as subjective reality constructed by actors participating in the interaction process rather than as objective reality (Hopf, 1998; Wendt, 1995). Evaluation of values, beliefs, and identities plays a crucial role in constructivist analysis as this analysis can allow explaining and predicting interstate behavior. According to Hopf (1998), subjective identities comprising beliefs, values, and ideals of state elites and populations define states' preferences and interests.

Constructivist literature emphasizes the fact that trust, collaboration, and politico-economic integration between states is possible when they identify with each other (Brown, 2005). When states as social actors do not identify with each other within the existing social structure, there will be revisionist and even revolutionary efforts that will lead to a conflict, the result of which will be a significant change in the social structure (Wendt, 1995).

As far as the landscape of international relations on the post-Soviet arena is concerned, Burant (1994) argued that important re-identification processes are typical of the post-Soviet space, where a new national consciousness is formed in the former socialist countries of Eastern and Central Europe. This new national consciousness is constructed through contrasting the values of the East European countries with those of Russia and through emphasizing the belonging of the Central and Eastern European countries to the Western civilization and Western structures such as the European Union and /or NATO and the United States. Fofanova and Morozov (2009) added that this new national consciousness varies by strength from the strongest in the Baltic states to the weakest in Belarus. This chapter aims to analyze how values and identities play a role in the current Russia-Ukrainian crisis. It also brings into the limelight the possibility for the competing identities internally, within a particular state that can also have an important effect on the structure and the content of international relations between states. The analysis conducted in this chapter also employs a generational perspective on the formation of domestic and foreign policy.

Analysis of Similarities and Differences in Value-based Systems

This chapter's analysis relies on two interrelated tracks of analysis: quantitative and qualitative. It relies on the combination of quantitative and qualitative methodological approaches to produce truly insightful results by combining statistical rigor with the rich detail of personal experiences communicated in the interviews. This two-prong approach gives a combination of rigor and richness of detail in the conveying of the value-based perspective of the current Russia-Ukraine crisis.

First, correlation analysis is applied to World Values Survey (WWS) data to analyze in a longitudinal manner similarities and differences in values between Russia and Ukraine with a particular focus on the last wave of WWS (2010–2014). This analysis also employs a generational perspective to examine possible differences in values at the generational level among the members of different generations of Russian and Ukrainian citizens. The second track of analysis relies on evaluation of in-depth interviews of government officials and representatives of different movements in order to examine their stance on the recent Russian-Ukraine crisis and to evaluate the differences in values, views, and beliefs between the Russians and the Ukrainians, as well as the underlying reasons for the two countries' behavior during the crisis.

Quantitative Analysis of Similarities and Differences in Values

To analyze differences and similarities in values systems of Russian and Ukrainian citizens, first, a correlation analysis of value categories (modeled as vector variables) was conducted using the last wave of World Value Survey (2010–2014). WWS represents a number of questions that are grouped into certain categories. Broadly, there are seventeen distinguishable categories that can be compared between Russia and Ukraine; each of these categories comprises a number of questions. A correlation analysis was conducted by modeling and correlating these categories as vector variables each consisting of a number of items. Table 4.1 presents the results of the analysis.

The correlations analysis indicates that overall, Russia and Ukraine are really similar in cultural, socioeconomic, and political values (total correlation is 0.81 with a high level of statistical significance). In such categories, as child upbringing values, family and male-female relationship values, work-related values, social position, these two countries are almost identical.

Table 4.1   Correlations in values/Russia and Ukraine

Values	Correlations
Things important in life	0.79***
Important child qualities	0.85***
Life satisfaction and happiness	0.93***
Individual qualities	0.88***
Work-related values	0.94***
Social position	0.90***
Justifiable	0.92***
Membership in organizations	0.61**
Worries	0.63***
Tolerance to differences and minorities	0.91***
Attitudes to male-female relationships and family values	0.96***
Aims of country	0.41***
Future changes	0.86***
Feeling as a nation	0.38*
Political action	0.59**
Satisfaction with institutions and trust in government and institutions	0.12
Political system and democracy	0.70***
Total	0.81***

Note: ***p < 0.01, **p < 0.05, *p < 0.1.

However, there are also important differences that exist in some categories that can shed light on why the Ukrainian Revolution took place and why such a serious conflict could take place between these two nations sharing common values in so many categories. This is the reason why the rest of the chapter will focus more on the value items stemming from the categories with low correlations. The categories with lowest correlations are membership in organizations (0.61), worries (0.63), feeling as a nation (0.38), national goals (0.41), political action (0.59), and satisfaction with institutions and trust in institutions (0.12, and insignificant correlation). Ukrainians appear to be more politically active than Russians (they give higher scores on questions related to signing petitions, participating in demonstrations, joining boycotts, etc.); they are also more often members of different organizations, including civil society organizations, and are generally less satisfied with the government and country's institutions than their Russian counterparts. Therefore, before the start of the conflict, the Ukrainians had been generally more prone to revolutionary actions than the Russians. The Ukrainians also do not see themselves as part of a nation as much as Russians, which has been used to explain the divide between the East and the West of Ukraine and secessionist tendencies in Eastern Ukraine in the aftermath of the conflict. Furthermore, the priorities of the national aims of the two countries are rather different.

To make a more nuanced analysis, a comparison of particular value items was carried out. Figures 4.1 and 4.2 present the results of this analysis.

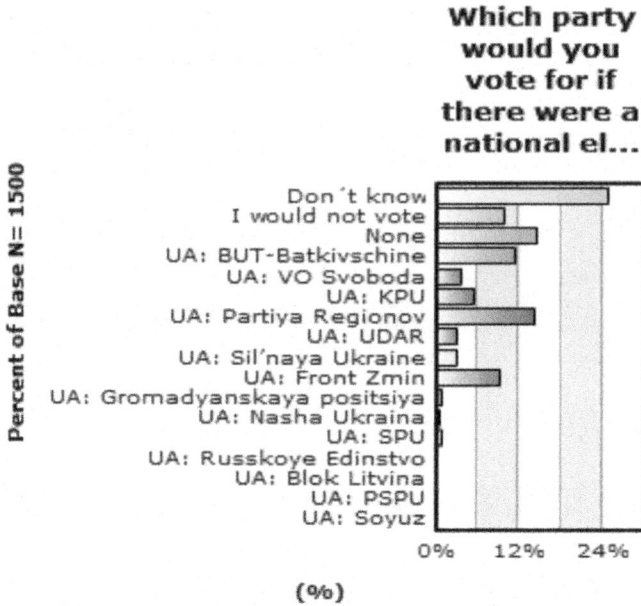

Figure 4.1   Values/Ukraine, 2010–2014 WVS Wave. Created by the authors from WVS Data.

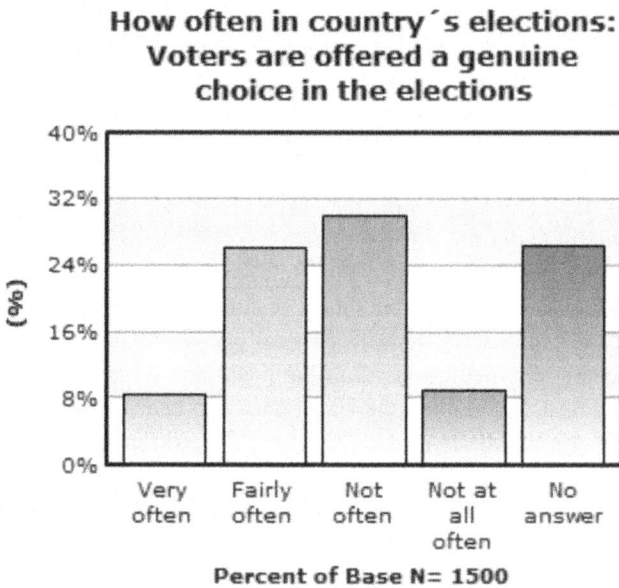

Figure 4.2   Values/Ukraine, 2010–2014 WVS Wave. Created by the authors from WVS Data.

I see myself as part of [CIS]

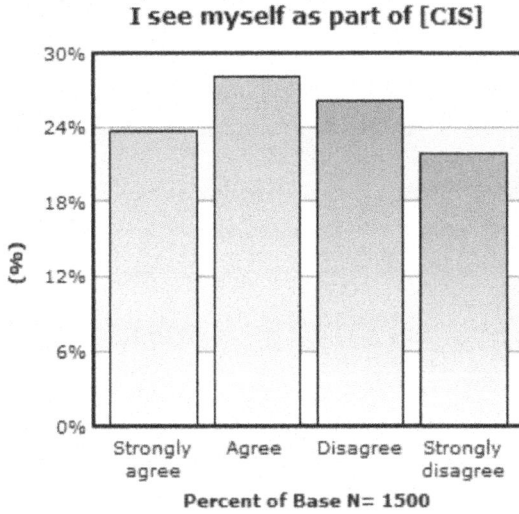

Percent of Base N= 1500

Figure 4.3   Values/Ukraine, 2010–2014 WVS Wave. Created by the authors from WVS Data.

Aims of Country: first choice

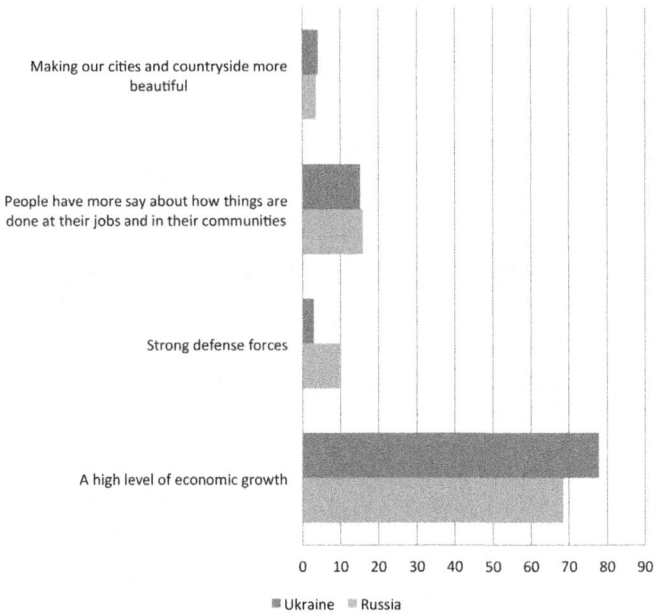

■ Ukraine   ■ Russia

Figure 4.4   Ukraine-Russia Value Comparisons, 2010–2014 WVS Wave. Created by the authors from WVS Data.

Attending peaceful demonstration

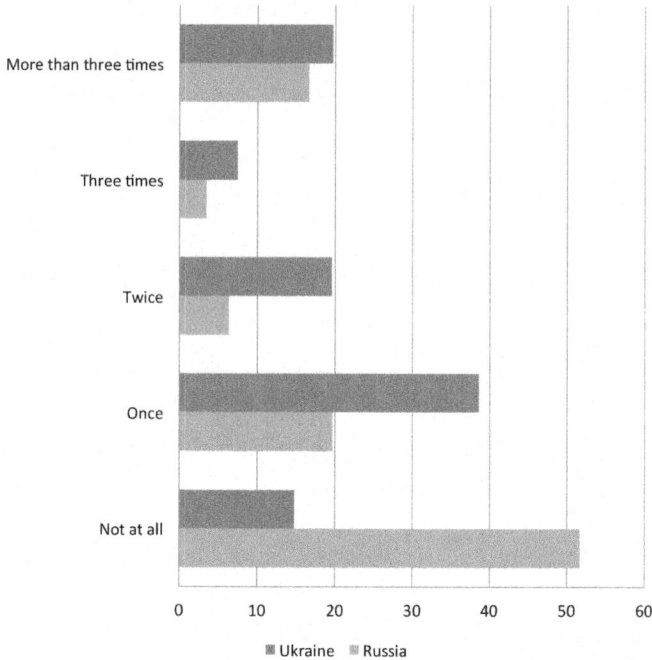

Figure 4.5   Ukraine-Russia Value Comparisons, 2010–2014 WVS Wave. Created by the authors from WVS Data.

The analysis indicates interesting differences: as far as country aims are concerned, the Ukrainians are more preoccupied with economic growth and are generally less concerned with the necessity of having strong defense. While for the Russians, too, economic growth is of higher importance than defense, they place more importance on having a strong defense system than their Ukrainian peers. Additionally, at the time of the survey the Ukrainians generally seem to feel more as a part of local community rather than as a part of a country, while Russians feel as part of a country as well as part of the Commonwealth of Independent States (CIS). It is interesting that while both the Russians and the Ukrainians fear a war that will include their country, the Ukrainians have more fears of civil war than the Russians. The events of the 2000s such as the Orange Revolution and the rise of the Party of Regions, as well as the presidential election of 2010, highlighted the adversarial politics of regional oligarchical clans. At the level of political voting there is a clear divide: before the conflict two very different parties Party of Regions (pro-Russian) and Batkivschina (pro-Western) had almost equal number of supporters (Figure 4.1).

Trusting institutions

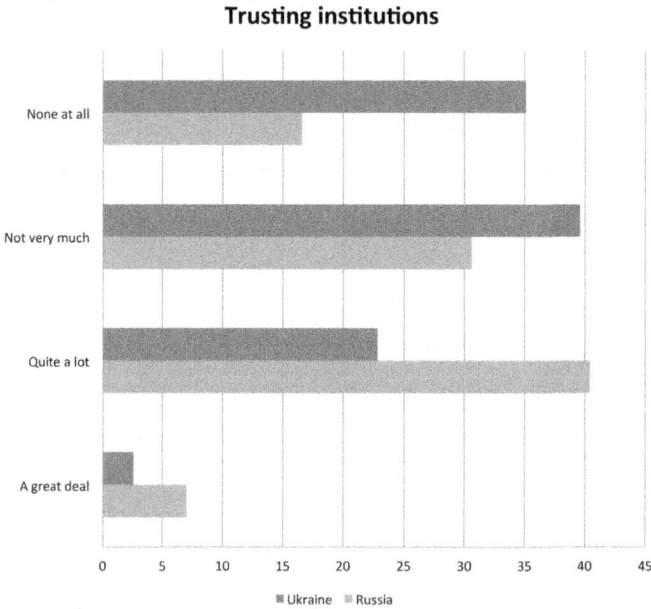

Figure 4.6   Ukraine-Russia Value Comparisons, 2010–2014 WVS Wave. Created by the authors from WVS Data.

Feeling as part of local community vs as part of a country

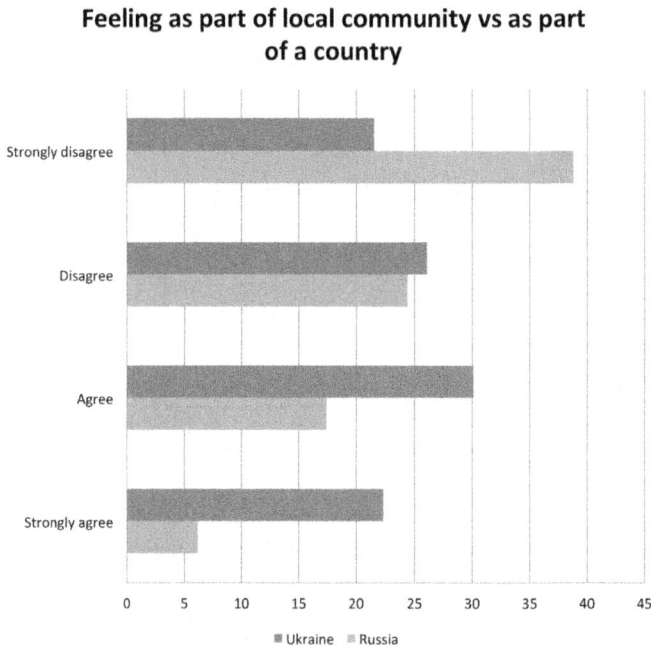

Figure 4.7   Ukraine-Russia Value Comparisons, 2010–2014 WVS Wave. Created by the authors from WVS Data.

Worries: a War Including my Country

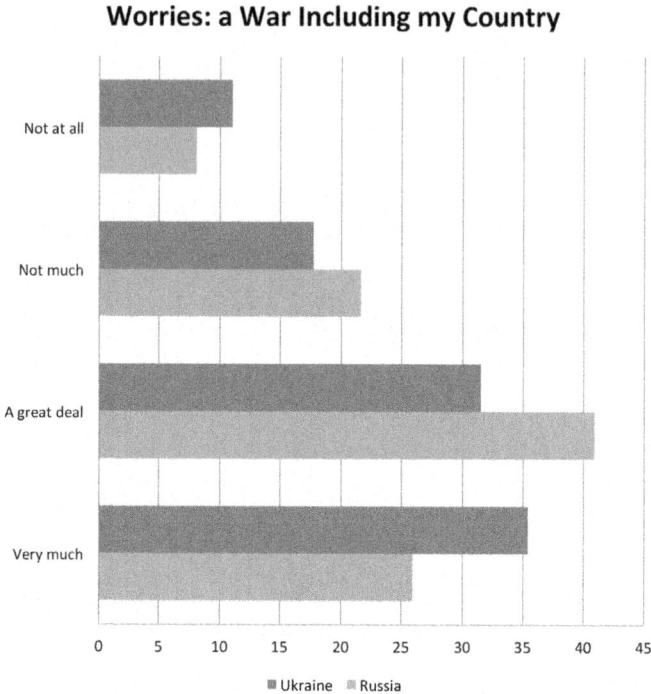

Figure 4.8   Ukraine-Russia Value Comparisons, 2010–2014 WVS Wave. Created by the authors from WVS Data.

It is also interesting to note Ukraine's deep mistrust in institutions in contrasting to Russia's relative confidence in institutions. These differences can explain why the majority of Russians did not share the revolutionary spirit of Maidan (the central square in Kyiv where the major protests occurred). It is also interesting that the Ukrainian society is divided as far as attitudes to the Commonwealth of Independent States are concerned: half of the population sees itself as part of the CIS, while the other half does not (Figure 4.1).

To capture the dynamics of change in values, two items across several waves of World Value Survey were compared: confidence in the government and cumulative confidence in country's institutions (courts, businesses, banks, etc.) (Figure 4.10).

The analysis indicates interesting trends. In Russia there is a general trend of increasing confidence in the government and in country's institutions: if in 1990s only 19% of the population was confident of the country's institutions, in 2010–2014, 53% were supportive of the country's institutions. The same trend is seen in the confidence the people have in the government. In Ukraine, on the other hand, in the 1990s, 27% of the population was satisfied with

Worries: Civil War in my Country

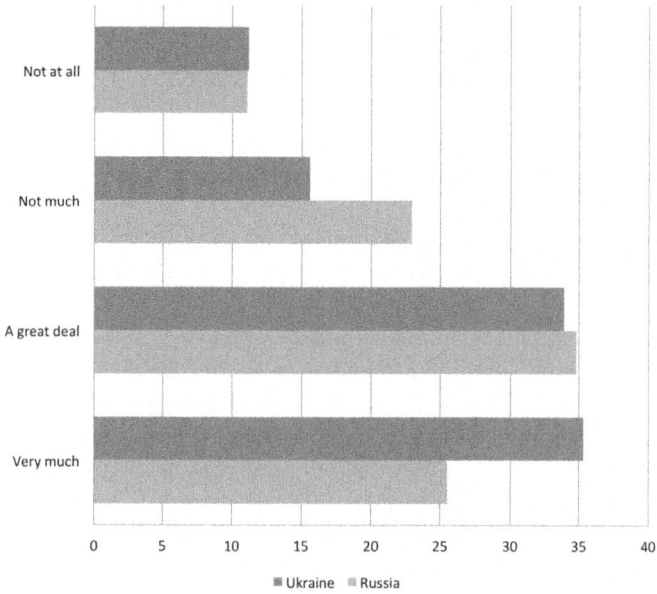

Figure 4.9   Ukraine-Russia Value Comparisons, 2010–2014 WVS Wave. Created by the authors from WVS Data.

Confidence in intistutions

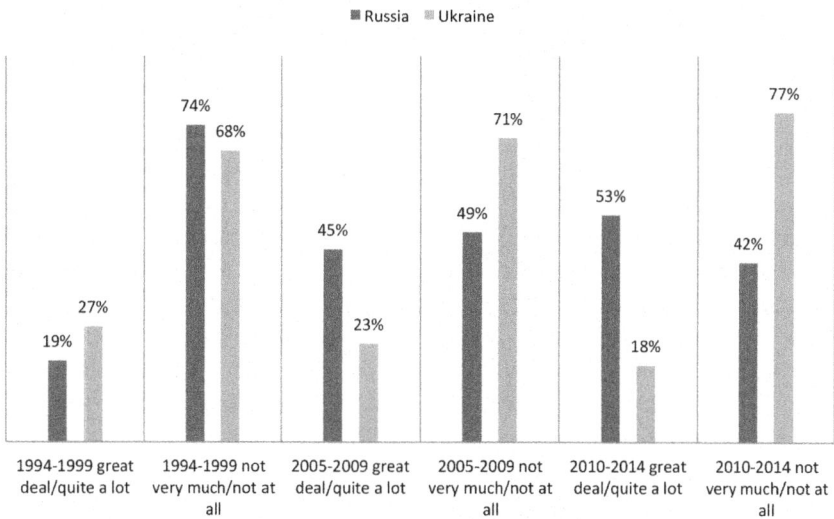

Figure 4.10   Change in Values. Created by the authors from WVS Data.

the country's institutions, while in 2010–2014, this figure dropped to 18%. Dissatisfaction with the institutions in Ukraine grew from 68% in the 1990s to 77% in 2010–2014. These results are not surprising as poor economic performance, political legacies of the postcommunist transition, as well as high levels of corruption undermined trust in state institutions (Mishelr and Rose, 1997, 2001; Wallace and Latcheva, 2006). The Kuchmagate scandal, the failures and disappointment of the Orange coalition, and the cynical kleptomaniac nature of the Yanukovych regime eroded the legitimacy and credibility of political elites and media in Ukraine to all-time lows by 2013. The same year Transparency International gave Ukraine a score of 25 and ranked it 144 our 177 on its corruption scale.[1]

This analysis reconfirms previous findings related to important differences between Russia and Ukraine in categories related to politics. While there is a strong correlation in the political system and democracy category, implying that both Russians and Ukrainians view democracy as a beneficial and viable perspective for the country's development and show similar responses on all the items in this category, they have different perception of the outcomes of the work of the government and the country's institutions. The Ukrainians felt over time that their government and institutions were increasingly nonrepresentative of the peoples' needs. This once again supports the findings about strong potential within the country for the revolution before it actually occurred.

These findings can also explain why according to the national-level survey conducted by USAID, in 2013 48% of the Ukrainian population were supportive of the Association with the European Union and thought it would positively affect the development of the country and would increase the standard of living of Ukrainian citizens.[2] The European Union is generally viewed as a progressive democratic polity and there is a general perception in the countries in the neighborhood (supported by academic research) that the European Union's institutions are effective and that Europeanization has positive politico-economic effects on the institutions in the neighborhood countries (Turkina and Surzhko-Harned, 2014). Therefore, the Ukrainians could have seen the Association with the European Union as a panacea against corruption and the malfunctioning of their country's institutions. What is more, the Association Agreement was one of the most anticipated promises of Yanukovych's 2010 presidential campaign. Yet, it is important to note, that while the disappointment with the Yanukovych decision not to sign the Association Agreement with the European Union might have been the spark that started the civil unrest in Ukraine, the Revolution of Dignity in Ukraine was a result of general dissatisfaction and increased anger with the Yanukovych government (Anders, 2014; Kuzio, 2015; Onuch, 2015; Surzhko-Harned and Zahuranec, 2017).

To make the analysis yet even more nuanced, a generation-level analysis of values was conducted based on 2010–2014 wave of World Value Survey. Table 4.2 presents the results of the regression analysis.

The results of the analysis indicate general commonalities between the first two generations; however, at the same time, there are also differences between the first two generations and third and the fourth generations of the Russians and the Ukrainians(especially between the first two generations and the fourth generations). The fourth generation of theUkrainians is very dissatisfied with the country's institutions, does not trust the government, and does not see itself as part of the Commonwealth of Independent States, and is more prone to participate in demonstrations than the other three generations. This may explain the marginalization of the Ukrainian youth and the participation of some young Ukrainians in radical movements such as the *Pravy Sector*. This can as well explain the fact that the driving force behind the Maidan movement was the Ukrainian youth. Unfortunately, there is no survey item on the attitudes toward the European Union and. especially, the Association with the European Union, but from the analysis carried out above and from the lack of support for the Commonwealth of Independent States from the fourth generation, unlike other generations, it is possible to deduce that the fourth generation is the strongest supporter of the Association Agreement with the European Union.

The next section will provide a deeper analysis of these findings through qualitative data based on interviews with Russia's officials and representatives of different movements in Russia.

INTERVIEWS

The following sections examines the values and beliefs of the Russian and Ukrainian political elite. The analysis is based on direct interviews, social media posts, press releases, and other public statements of the political elite in both Russian and Ukraine. The differences in values, beliefs, and views mentioned by the respondents that play a role in the current Russia-Ukraine crisis can be divided into three broad interconnected categories: security and geopolitics-related values, economic values and attitudes to the government and institutions, and socio-cultural values. We organize the analysis along these categories for each of the countries.

The Russian Side of the Story

This section is based on 11 in-depth interviews conducted over the period of September–October 2014 with representatives of different parties in Russia

Table 4.2 Probability analysis of values

	Participation in demonstrations (Ukraine)	Feeling as part of CIS (Ukraine)	Satisfaction with institutions and trust in the government (Ukraine)	Participation in demonstrations (Russia)	Feeling as part of CIS (Russia)	Satisfaction with institutions and trust in the government (Russia)
	Coefficient/SE	Coefficient/SE	Coefficient/SE	Coefficient/SE	Coefficient/SE	Coefficient/SE
Generation 1	-0.521***	0.451***	0.298***	-0.481***	0.701***	0.113***
	(0.003)	(0.022)	(0.001)	(0.001)	(0.002)	(0.001)
Generation 2	-0.217***	0.222***	0.302***	-0.395***	0.685***	0.336***
	(0.008)	(0.009)	(0.002)	(0.007)	(0.001)	(0.001)
Generation 3	0.003***	-0.002*	-0.244***	-0.004***	0.332*	-0.008
	(0.001)	(0.001)	(0.001)	(0.001)	(0.001)	(0.009)
Generation 4	0.219***	-0.307***	-0.699***	0.002***	0.118***	0.105***
	(0.001)	(0.002)	(0.001)	(0.001)	(0.002)	(0.001)
Education	0.136***	-0.449	-0.003**	0.136***	0.004***	-0.001***
	(0.027)	(0.548)	(0.001)	(0.027)	(0.001)	(0.001)
N	1,008	1,008	1,008	1,474	1,474	1,474
Pseudo R^2	0.0572	0.0483	0.0495	0.0591	0.0446	0.5992

Note: *p < .10, **p < .05, ***p < .01.

(CPRF (communist) Party, Democratic Party, Just Party, and United Russia Party), as well as representatives of different Russian movements, including the opposition movement "Bolotnaya white ribbon movement." The interviews provide more detail regarding the human experiences of the current Russia-Ukraine conflict and people's beliefs about how differences in values, views, and beliefs can play a role in the current divide. They also offer an invaluable insight into the process of political change though the eyes of the activists and decision-makers.

The interviews were conducted in a semi-structured format consisting of a set of core questions supplemented by an in-depth discussion about different subjects the respondent was willing to provide further detail about. All the interviews were conducted in the Russian language and were translated into English. Open/axial/core coding method developed by Anselm Strauss was applied to process and codify information contained in the interviews (Strauss, 1997).

Security and Geopolitics-related Values

All the respondents agree that the Russians and the Ukrainians have different attitudes to the overall geopolitical situation and security-related issues, which is reflected in different stances on the WVS questions related to the attitudes to the Commonwealth of Independent States, worries of the war, and the civil war that would include the respondents' countries. For instance, a representative of the Just Party shares:

> Russia is deeply concerned with NATO expansion to the East and different officials have voiced their concerned at different international events many times. Before the dissolution of the Warsaw pact, Gorbachev was explicitly promised non-expansion of NATO to the East, but the promise was breached. We see bases in the Baltic countries and new systems deployed in Poland and Czech Republic. Of course, we do not buy the arguments that these moves are against Iran as any sensible person understanding geography knows what the purpose of those missiles in Eastern Europe is to cover the European territory of Russia. We also see that the United States unilaterally exited several important accords, ABM Treaty being one of them. All these moves and the lack of willingness to cooperate (yes, there was this NATO-Russia Partnership for Peace Program, but it was more symbolic rather than real cooperation), left us with impression that while we give up strategic positions (for instance, by complying with the CFE (Conventional Forces in Europe) Treaty), the U.S. already has the agreements signed with both Romania and Bulgaria in 2006 that specifically allow for permanent bases under direct U.S. control. This is a clear violation of the CFE Treaty, but does anyone in the West care? Why am I talking about all this? To place the conflict with the Ukraine in a broader geopolitical context. All the developments between Russia and the West that I have talked about happened

long before the conflicts with Georgia and with Ukraine. Now, both Ukraine and Georgia voiced out their desire to join NATO. There have already been several joint trainings, for example marine events in Sevastopol. So, the alliance that should have been dissolved together with the Warsaw Pact will now be at the border of Russia?

Many interviewees claimed that Russia and Ukraine have different views on their geopolitical objectives. For instance, the same representative of the Just Party argued:

While Russia is concerned with securing its borders and reconstructing itself as a regional power and ultimately perceives its near abroad as its security and polity continuum, I think Ukraine sees itself as both part of a Russian World, but also increasingly as part of Western structures, especially the European Union. While Russia, in general, has less concern over the EU expansion than NATO expansion, given the rudimentary common security and defense policy of the EU, in the matters related to international relations, NATO is its point of reference in Europe as the EU countries are also NATO members. ... I believe this overlapping geopolitical identity of the Ukrainians (part of society sees itself as part of the Russian world, the other part sees itself more belonging to Western civilization) plays a role in the current juxtaposition between its southern and eastern provinces and the central government with its Western agenda. If we speak about war threat, for Russians it is more an external concern and perception of external threat, while for Ukrainians it is largely internal concern exactly because of this overlapping identity. Of course, Russia plays an important role in the Ukraine's internal affairs by backing up the separatists pursuing its security objectives of supporting the creation of buffer zones between Russia and pro-Western polity, but without the internal division of society and overlapping identities in Ukraine this would not be possible.

In general, all the respondents (even from the opposition movement) agree that Ukraine became the battleground for Russian and Western interests and that Russia is currently redefining itself as a regional power influenced by the old legacies of the Russian Empire and the Soviet Union. A representative of KPRF party argues:

This geopolitical struggle for Ukraine did not happen yesterday; it has its roots in the so called the Great Game, the strategic rivalry and conflict between the British Empire and the Russian Empire for supremacy in Eurasia. Since then, the West has been constantly interfering with the Russia's backyard and threatening its core strategic interests. The most recent developments include financing the anti-Russia movements and the so-called color revolutions along the perimeter of Russia. For example, Madame Nuland (the U.S. assistant secretary of state for European and Eurasian affairs), openly admitted that the United States had invested more than $5 billion to help Ukraine achieve "the future it deserves." I personally do not think it is because of genuine and idealist democracy-driven considerations, I think it is soft power politics that aims at defending strategic objectives in the region. At least Russia perceives it this way and does not like this interference. Soft power politics is not as visible as direct interference, but nonetheless, very productive. While after the collapse of the Soviet Union, Russia has been focused on redefining itself, the new generation of Ukrainians became heavily influenced by western ideas, culture; they have new perception of history that also came from re-written history books in schools sponsored by the West including Soros-funded educational programs. As a result, we have a new generation of Ukrainians, especially in Western Ukraine, who is very different from the older generations that shared a similar Soviet experience. It is very difficult to us (Russian politicians) to communicate with those young guys who took places in Rada after the 2014 coup, because they do not share with us the same understanding of history and the same understanding of geopolitics. At the same time, a part of our Russian youth is also rather westernized and liberalized. So, sometimes we have hard times understanding them too.

Another responded added:

Over these thirty years, Russia has been struggling to re-identify itself and did not pay much attention to soft instruments in its near abroad. If to speak about Russian post-Soviet identity, Russia has experienced a dramatic challenge of forming a new identity as it had a strong basis of the legacies of the Russian Empire and those of the Soviet Union that needed to be reconciled and included in the new identity. The challenge here is that both the Russian Empire and the Soviet Union had regional identities based on administering vast territories and diverse populations. After the fall of the USSR, the territory of Russia shrank and Russia had to go through the process of nation consolidation or choosing a nation-state-based identity. At the same time, that overlapping regional identity and previous legacies have always been there like a phantom. I believe this is why especially in security domain Russia still considers its "near abroad" as a continuity of its interests vis-à-vis its old adversaries of the Great Game epoch and the US, who is viewed by Russia as a continuation of the Anglo-Saxon pole in world politics and international relations.

At the same time, respondents argue that Ukraine too has struggled to define its national geopolitical aspirations and these identification processes clash with those occurring in Russia. For instance, a representative of the opposition movement argues:

Post-Soviet Ukraine had to build its own identity and with western support it redefined itself partially as in opposition to Russia. For instance, I remember how Chernovil (opposition leader) and other opposition leaders criticized Kuchma

(Ukrainian president) for agreeing to let the Russian military base in Crimea to stay until 2017. That was long before the conflict, the relationship between the countries was good back then, but still Ukrainian opposition believed that Kuchma was serving Russia's imperialistic interests. Therefore, shortly after the collapse of the Soviet Union part of national elites representing part of the population in Ukraine were already identifying Ukrainian geopolitical interests in negation to those of Russia. Of course, this identification was bound to clash with that of Russia. There is another side of the story with Sevastopol, as well as many other cities in South-Eastern Ukraine founded by the Russian Empire polity, forming an important part of Russia's history and geopolitical identity. Therefore, with Ukraine potentially joining NATO, Russia would suddenly have to face the part of its heritage under control of its ancient foes, which I think would be a painful attack on its identity. Russia was very upset with NATO bases in the Baltics; Russia does share common history with the Baltic countries that were controlled by the Russian empire and then by the Soviet Union, but still they were different polities and Russian leaders did not found cities there; while Sevastopol is the "glorious city of Russian marines," Odessa founded by Catherine the Great, etc. … It is like to bite of St Petersburg from the Russian map. … I am exaggerating of course, but the parallel is clear.

The respondents also mentioned legal aspects related to the transfer of the Crimea to Ukraine that played a role in the conflict. For example, a representative of the opposition movement shared:

The problem here is also mistakes with the transfer of the Crimea to Ukrainian SSR. According to article 33 of the constitution, Khrushchev did not have the authority to do the transfer unilaterally, and the constitution was subsequently changed to accommodate the transfer. Moreover, in 1992 the Supreme Soviet of Russia claimed that the transfer was illegitimate. Nonetheless, in 1997 Russia recognized territorial integrity of Ukraine, so we as opposition believe that instead of falling in realpolitik with Crimean annexation and fierce confrontation, Russia should have used softer instruments to deal with the situation. The arguments given by the supporters of the annexation is that it is hypocritical of the USA and the EU to say that Russia did not observe international law when the US and its allies breached international law so many times. But I and my other opposition colleagues think that power politics will lead nowhere and will be very costly in terms of human lives.

Another respondent from the same opposition movement added:

If we speak about identity, both Russia and Ukraine experience a complicated re-identification process. While for Russia the main challenge is to develop a national identity that would also comprise its empirical and Soviet heritage, for Ukraine the main challenge is to bridge the sharp identity divide between its

Western and Central provinces on the one side, and the Southern and Eastern ones on the other. All the evidence including different value surveys show that Western Ukrainians are Anti-Soviet, view Russia as an enemy while the US as a major ally, support the entry of Ukraine into the EU and NATO. At the same time, Eastern Ukrainians exhibit opposite values and geopolitical orientations: they see themselves as part of the Common Wealth of Independent States, support entry into the customs union with Russia, Belarus, Kazakhstan, and Armenia. If we take a look at the youngest generation that were educated in the post-Soviet period under significant western influence, then even in the East we can find some support for integration with the EU and appreciation of US. ... So, I believe younger generations of Western and South-Eastern Ukrainians share more in common than their parents and grandparents. However, I think with after the current internal conflict we will, unfortunately, see even the Ukrainian youth very polarized too as the South-Easterners see their families and friends killed in the counter-operation and will have problems with forgiving these losses, while the Westerners will have hard times reconciling with the separatist tendencies in the South-East.

While the interviewees have different opinions of Russia's re-identification as a regional power and its interference in the neighborhood (representatives of the opposition movement think Russia should use softer instruments to promote its interests in the neighborhood, while the members of the leading parties support more aggressive moves to ensure the country's security and defend its geostrategic interests vis-à-vis expanding the European Union and especially NATO), all the respondents share an opinion that it would be safer for Ukraine to have a more inclusive approach to its identity building process that would be able to bridge the values of its Western and South-Eastern population.

Economic and Institutional Values

As far as economic and institutional values are concerned, the respondents noted a similar clash between Russia and Ukraine, as well as between the Western and South-Eastern provinces of Ukraine.
A representative of the Democratic Party argued:

Economic identity of Russia is based on positioning itself as an emerging economy, as well as an orchestrator of Eurasian integration that would be a counterpart to other major blocks such as the EU, in particular, and NAFTA. Indeed, it has been proven that it is easier to compete in the current economy as a block rather than individually. Given that Russia does not have aspirations to join the EU, it makes more sense for it to develop alternative economic structures in Eurasia. At the same time, Ukrainian economic model and economic identity is really split between on the one hand, having close business relations

with Russia, sharing common business networks, having cross-border enter-
prises, common banking activities, and at the same time, economic aspirations
of joining the EU in the long-run. It is interesting that while in practice Ukraine
is much tighter connected with Russia at the level of business elites than with
the EU and eagerly takes Russian low percent credits and other types of financial support, but at the political level in the long run it sees itself increasingly as
part of the EU-led economic schemes.

A representative of United Russia Party added:

> We really have to speak about values here. From pure economic standpoint the
> Association with the EU would not be as beneficial for the Ukrainian economy
> as Maidan supporters think. I am an economist by education and with a western
> degree, so I know what I am talking about. First, to benefit from any trade and
> investment liberalization agreement in a particular sector, a country has to have
> a competitive advantage in this sector. Now, the EU is clearly more advanced
> than Ukraine in all the sectors of the economy. And if we take agriculture, we
> all know that with subsidies under the EU CAP policy it is not possible to gain
> any benefits for external parties. The heavy and light industries in Ukraine
> will be inevitably destroyed or overtaken by foreign capital. If we analyze the
> losses from similar association agreement with Algeria on any other country
> in the neighborhood, we will see that Ukraine will certainly not benefit in
> the short and medium term, and doubtful in the long run. Rushing to sign the
> Association Agreement without gradual preparation and the adjacent reforms
> will put Ukrainian economy on the knees. That is why Yatsenyuk hesitated to
> sign the economic part of the agreement, even though he had heavily criticized
> Yanukovych for diversion from the Association agreement to the customs
> union with Russia. For instance, in addition to the problems stemming from
> very skewed economic relationships between the EU and Ukraine, there were
> important technical requirements; for instance, Ukraine had to conduct a rail-
> road infrastructure reform to meet European standards, a very costly project,
> and at its own expense. However, the majority did not read the agreement. I
> highly doubt that even a small percentage of Maidan revolutionists thoroughly
> analyzed the content of the agreement. For Maidan public these purely eco-
> nomic considerations did not play any role. Western Ukrainians and some
> supporters of the Revolution from the youngest generation from the East did
> not care about any sustentative analyses. For them the value of the Association
> was very irrational as it was based on the symbolism of being with the "pros-
> perous, developed, and democratic EU" and not with "economically emerging
> and autocratic Russia."

Several respondents also argued that they believe that majority of Ukrainians
do not understand that the association agreement is not a guaranteed path
to membership. According to the interviewees, from a purely economic

standpoint it is an effort to neoliberalize Ukraine in accordance with Western interests such as opening a lucrative market for the European Union, but it is not clear if Ukraine will be economically healthier being part of the Agreement. The interviewees claimed that Ukraine was forced to choose to join either the Agreement or the customs union. One of the respondents shared:

> The Association Agreement will inevitably hinder Ukraine-Russia economic relations. ... At the same time, people in the South-East of Ukraine were more supportive of the customs union with Russia than the Association with the EU again, not because of some purely economic considerations, but because of their politico-economic values and perceptions of the necessity to be with the customs union.

Many respondents also mentioned important differences in the institutional values of Russians and Ukrainians.

A representative of Just Russia shared:

> The transition of the 1990s was so painful for Russia that when Putin came to power and the country started to increase its economic performance, the majority of the population were happy to close eyes on high corruption, institutional problems (e.g., malfunctioning of courts) and the lack of some freedoms in exchange for economic stability. Of course, oil money was important in stabilizing and giving push to the Russian economy, but I have always argued that it is highly important to diversify the economy, conduct the necessary reforms, etc. At the same time, the Ukrainians did not have the luxury of high oil prices and in general, having high profits from natural resource rents and were much more affected by the inefficiency of their institutions. In Ukraine basically powerful politico-business elites continued to rob the general population. We have more confidence of our institutions ... even though in practice their quality leaves much to be desired ... because the general standards of living have been increasing and some social initiatives did take place such as maternity capital, daycare reform, etc. In Ukraine, all this was absent and dissatisfaction with the country's government and institutions lead to increasing revolutionary attitudes in the society. I believe if Russia managed to fully diversify its economy, combat corruption, conduct democratic reforms, it would have been a better role model, but given the current state of affairs and comparing Russia's institutions with those in the EU, many Ukrainians believe that rapprochement with the EU is healthier and more beneficial, since it can affect the existing clan-based business and politics and reduce corruption. This is, however, not applied to business elites in South-Eastern Ukraine who benefited from institutional malfunctions. I will give a few examples, but not for the record. ... For them, connectedness to Russia and existing business ties are far more important than potential EU-induced institutional reforms conducted by the central government. So, again we speak

about important internal identity split. … Even among the Ukrainian oligarchs
we see a clear divide between those who support the Russian regional economic
model and those who ardently support the Association with the EU

Another responded from United Russia Party nuanced:

All parts of Ukraine are similar in this important aspect: the dominant social
group in all regions now consists of "oligarchs," those who made fortunes by
exploiting their close political connections and appropriating state-owned assets
at cheap prices. Just to give an idea of how important they are, about just fifty
oligarchs control more than eighty five percent of Ukrainian GDP. And about
nighty percent of them have their backgrounds in organized crime. They own
businesses, mass media, and control all the current political parties. Now, these
oligarchs are also divided along the same geopolitical and economic lines. At
present, there are rival clans and I can easily name those who are pro-Russian
and those who are pro-Western. Pro-Western believe Association Agreement
will help them to secure their interests vis-à-vis the pro-Russian clans, while
the pro-Russian clans feel their fortuned will be more secured in the union with
Russia. Since both groups control mass media, they do have a very heavy influence on the perceptions, attitudes, and value formation of the general population. Unfortunately, since the collapse of the USSR the Ukraine has been like
a blanket pulled into two different sides and all the oligarchs and politicians
played well on the West-East identity divide. I think this is one of the main
factors that led to such a heated internal conflict. There was hardly any figure
with centralist approach that would be based on inclusive elements and bridge
the West and the South-East.

In general, while all the respondents agreed that the economic costs of
the Association Agreement might outweigh the benefits in the short and
medium term, practically all of them mentioned the symbolism of the Association as an instrument to withdraw (even painfully and at high cost for the
general population and especially for some business elites) from the Russian
economic and institutional orbit and drastically cut the ties existing between
the current business elites, as well as small and medium-sized businesses.
Of course, this goes on in the clash with Russia's economic projections in
the region as an alternative economic block. The situation is aggravated
by the fact that having high degree of interconnectedness, Russia will inevitably bear losses from losing the Ukrainian market and economy to another
block.

Socio-cultural Values

As far as sociocultural values are concerned, all the respondents mentioned
them as important factors in explaining the current crisis as cultural identity

and foreign policy go hand in hand and domestic and foreign policies are closely linked. In addition to mentioning the famous tensions between the Slavophils and the Westerners, many respondents also spoke about other competing cultural narratives currently persisting in Russia: Russian Europeanness and Russia as a separate civilization. In both narratives, Ukraine is very important.

As one responded from the Civic Chamber shared:

> Kiev and Ukraine are key to Russian Europeanness. The first capital of the Russian polity was Novgorod Veliky. Then in 882 Novgorod Prince Oleg freed Kiev from Khazar rule and transferred the capital into Kiev. Kievan Rus became a prosperous and vast (in terms of territory) Russian State that actively traded with Europe and was an inalienable part of the European landscape of the medieval times. Even though without Ukraine Russia will still have its European roots embodied in Novgorod that was a very progressive democratic polity at its foundation, as well as St Petersburg and all the family linkages between Russian Rurik and Romanov dynasties and European aristocracy, but still Ukraine and Kiev are crucially important for the Russian European identity. As far as the second Russian narrative concerned, it is the story of a grand civilization on its own. Here we speak about Russia as a grand civilization with Moscow being the Third Rome. In this second vision spirituality and religion are very important and the well-being of the Russian citizens is considered to be directly related to the well-being of the State. In this vision Kievan Rus is also very symbolic, because it is associated with the roots of Russian Orthodoxy.

Several respondents argued that modern Ukraine is perceived by Russia as a continuation of the so-called Russian World. Another respondent from the Democratic Party spoke about Eurasianism and Nationalism as competing narratives for the Russian identity.

> From the literature and history we see two competing visions of Russian identity, namely Eurasianism and Nationalism. Eurasianists believe that Russia is a civilization on its own with Russians as a titular ethnic group, but also comprising many ethnic groups. The Eurasionist vision in geopolitics translates into the perception of Russia as a specific orbit, around which smaller nations rotate. In this vision Russia is a regional actor rather, not a simple nation state. In this vision Ukraine is important as it is perceived as belonging to the Russian orbit, Russian civilization. Eurasionist vision also focuses on the idea of cyclical development rather than neoliberal linear progress. Eurasionists believe that social organization is bound to repetition and institutions repeat and reproduce similar development trajectories. Therefore, civilization needs strong culture and strong moral foundations, since institutions are repetitive and are rather the outcome of culture than vice versa. In this vision civilization also needs strong

administrative rule and strong regional identity, because they will help to govern immense geography.

According to this respondent, this Eurasionist vision is very different from the Nationalist vision, as nationalism focuses on the cultural unity of Russians. The respondents mentioned an interesting divide among current Russian nationalists as some nationalists focus on the Slavic origin of the Russians and pan-Slavism and, therefore, the need to cooperate with other Slavs and develop pan-Slavic formation, while the others focus on ethnic Russians and their differences from other ethnic groups, including other Slavs. One of the interviewees shared:

> Some Russian ultranationalists perceived the developments in South-Eastern Ukraine as a struggle and a long-term conflict between ethnic Russians and Ukrainian nationalists, or in other words, "Banderists." Some believe the conflict is between ethnic Russians, some of whom have been subjected to cultural and linguistic "Ukrainization" supported by the West and therefore, lost their identity.

According to the respondents, the majority of the Russian Nationalists believe that Putin is genuinely defending Russian and pan-Slavic interests in the region against the West. Many Eurasionists support this point of view thinking that Putin is defending Eurasionist values. At the same time, there is also a group of nationalists who disapprove of Russia's current position toward Ukraine as they believe that the overthrow of Yanukovych was more a revolution against corruption rather than ethnic conflict. There are also Westerners and Russian liberal elites adhering to the European identity of Russia and share the same opinion that harsh moves against Ukraine can be explained by the fear of the current regime in Russia that a similar revolution may happen in Moscow. Westerners also fear that the conflict with Ukraine may be used to distract the population from the lack of political freedoms in Russia, to raise Putin's personal approval ratings, as well as the ratings of the United Russia Party.

As far as the Ukrainian cultural identity projected in foreign policy is concerned, the respondents also noted competing narratives that can explain the magnitude of the current clash.

A representative of the Civic Chamber argued:

> I can differentiate between the two-main national-level narratives in the identity of the modern-day Ukraine. Though both narratives emphasize Ukraine uniqueness, one is clearly based on the linkages with Russia, common history starting from Kievan Rus and ending with the common communist and then

transition experience. The second one emphasizes that Ukraine is absolutely different from Russia, rejects to recognize that Russia descends from Kievan Rus and actually juxtaposes the "enlightened" Kievan Rus to the "autocratic and despotic" Grand Dutchy of Moscow and then the Russian Empire, views the Ukrainian Soviet experience through the prism of occupation. In this narrative Russia is perceived as the opposite of democratic and civilized Europe. In this narrative Russia exploited Ukraine to achieve its power ambitions. It is interesting that in this narrative there is even no place for the enlightened and democratic Novgorod Republic that was a much more democratically advanced polity than any of its European contemporaries. When I ask the Ukrainian ultranationalists about Novgorod Republic from where the whole formation of East-Slavic polity took place inevitably placing us (Ukrainians and Russians) in a common history, they always shrug their shoulders and do not know what to answer. Now, these two different narratives translate into different approaches to foreign and domestic policy formation: one glorifies Soviet Union victory in the Second World War (called the Great Patriotic War), the other rejects the notion of the "Great Patriotic War" and views World War II as a struggle between two totalitarian regimes with Ukraine being exploited and being in the middle. One praises the achievements of the Russian Empire and then those of the Soviet Union and the Red Army and has an anti-heroic vision of Bandera's deeds, the other emphasizes Holodomor and Soviet oppression and praises Bandera as a national hero. Of course, this second narrative goes in severe clash with all the narratives that are part of the Russian identity."

A respondent from the opposition movement added:

Even as a Russian who wholeheartedly supports the westernization and the liberalization of Russia and who was at the roots of the DPR party initiative to make a referendum in Russia for joining the EU, I was deeply sad about drastic attacks on Soviet-era symbols (destruction of monuments), the Russian language, etc. shortly after Maidan revolution. I think this transformation should have been much more gradual. Otherwise it really scared and alienated the population in the South-East of Ukraine who were quite ambivalent about Maidan, but who also nevertheless disapproved corruption and in principle would not mind removing Yanoukovich from power. Suddenly from silent observers and even sometimes supporters of the revolution these populations turned into defensive stance and became largely supportive of separatism. I strongly believe that the revolution for democracy should look into future and conduct the necessary political and economic reforms rather than engage in history revisionist work that would attack the cultural narrative of half of the country's population.

While all the interviewees see the inevitable clash between the narratives of the Russian and the Ukrainian identities, many of them hope that the younger generations in both countries will be able to bridge this divide.

As the representative of the Just Russia Party argued:

Despite differences in the vision of the counties' development paths, I think younger generations of Russians and Ukrainians who lived through the same post-Soviet transition process, who had a chance to travel and to see the world can serve as a bridge to heal the current divide between Russia and Ukraine. These younger generations are creative, place value in civil society, mobility, have progressive views on different categories of values, master technology and social networking. For instance, I see a lot of similarities between Moscow youth and young people in Lviv (I had a chance to meet young people there at some events). I am not talking here about far-right nationalists who are equally scary in Ukraine and in Russia. Sadly, in Ukraine they managed to get some small access to the country's institutional environment, but I hope they will not stay there after several rounds of elections and reforms. But I am talking about educated, progressive, open-minded, but at the same time patriotic and respectful youth who can find a way to reconcile and ease the current agony. For instance, my son has friends in Ukraine via on-line social networking. They have their clubs, meetings, etc. They keep dialogue even in the current difficult situation. I think the worst thing that can happen is losing the dialogue. I believe younger generations are the key to finding a way out.

The Ukrainian Side of the Story

The Ukrainian side of the story is told through the analysis of the public statement made by the political and social leaders of Ukraine between 2014 and 2016. We looked at official websites, press releases, media reports, and social media posts of such leaders as President Perto Proshenko, former prime minister Arseniy Yatsenuk, leader of the Radical Party Oleg Lyashko, parliamentarian from Batkivshchina Party and social leader Nadiya Savchenko, and parliamentarians from the Opposition Block among others.

Security and Geopolitics

Among Ukrainian political elite there is a general consensus the Revolution of Dignity brought about the necessary impetus for much-needed change. Most believe that Ukraine is a European nation whose citizens deserve to live in the prosperous democratic country free of corruption.

The official position of the Ukrainian government does not recognize the Referendum in Crimea and holds that Crimea is Ukraine. President Proshenko vowed to preserve Ukraine's territorial integrity and sovereignty. Moreover, most Ukrainian politicians hold that the separatists fighting the Ukrainian armed forces in the Donbas region are sponsored and supported by the Russian Federation. Verkhovna Rada, as well as, the office of the president and Ministry of Interior bluntly stated that there is indisputable evidence of Russia's involvement in the East. On the second anniversary of the so-called referendum in Crimea, Proshenko addressed the world with the following statement:

> Crimea was, is and will be an integral part of the Ukrainian state and the country-criminal will be forced to return the loot. Sooner or later, this will happen no matter how long the de-occupation of the peninsula will last. It is natural that Ukraine does not recognize and will never de jure recognize residents of the peninsula who received Russian passports as Russian citizens. Russian citizens do not live in Crimea. It is inhabited only by Ukrainian citizens. Our people live on our territory, which is temporarily occupied.
>
> Until the return of Crimea to its historically determined place within Ukraine, our key task is to protect citizens' rights and freedoms in Crimea and provide support to any source of legitimate resistance to the Russian occupants and their local "goblins-puppets."[3]

The Ukrainian military helicopter pilot-turned-politician and member of Parliament Nadiya Savchenko, who was captured, arrested, and tried in the show trial by the Russian Federation, spoke passionately in court on March 3, 2016.

> The guilt of Russian-backed separatist forces and Russian regular military troops has also been proven. They are guilty of killing Ukrainian people on our Ukrainian land. They are to blame for occupying Ukrainian lands. Let the Donbas' so-called "peace-loving residents," victims and separatists scream as loud as they can that it was only they who were are being killed by Ukraine's armed forces. Even the video provided by Yegor Rossiysky [a Russian journalist] proved the opposite and showed separatists beating and killing Ukrainian prisoners of war.
>
> This court also proved the FSB (Security Service) and Russia's Investigative Committee guilty. They are to blame for kidnapping people. They are guilty of torturing people. The group of [Ukrainian prisoners being held in Russia] Sentsov, Karpyuk and Klykh were tortured. These services and committees are to blame for trying, bad-mouthing and accusing those they kidnap and torture. These services and committees forge expert findings, and this was proved.[4]

Ukrainian's former prime minister Arseniy Yatsenyuk in his press conference with the US vice president Joe Biden on April 22, 2014, said:

> Let me reiterate the position of the Ukrainian government once again. Never, under no circumstance Ukraine would acknowledge the annexation of Crimea. We will require from our Russian neighbors to immediately get their special forces out of the eastern region of Ukraine, so get its military

forces from Crimea, thus closing down this ignoble page in history of occupation of our territory by the Russian troops. We believe that in this century
and in the modern world, no country should be allowed to behave like an
armed bandit.

And it's inadmissible, especially for those countries who are standing members of the Security Council of the United Nations. And it's inadmissible to a
country that used to be a member of G8. Russia should stick to its international
commitments and obligations. We are not asking anything from Russia. What
we demand from them is one thing and only, they should deliver on the international commitments, and they should not behave as gangsters in the modern
century.[5]

The precarious position of Ukraine locked in the conflict with Russia did not
result from Ukraine being caught in the middle of the geopolitical game of
West vs. Russia, rather it is a position of crossroads between a democratic
and accountable form of governance and Soviet-style authoritarianism. In his
statement at the High-Level Leaders' Roundtable "Political Leadership to
Prevent and End Conflicts" in Istanbul on May 23, 2016, President Proshenko
said:

It's not a hostility between "the west" and "the rest."

It's the hostility between those who seek harmony and those who seek
domination.

It's the hostility between those who play by the rules and those who believe
that the rules don't really exist.

We see it very clearly in today's Russia—a nuclear nation that sees democracy as a threat and freedom as a poison.

This situation is not about a different interpretation.

It's about different goals.

The west seeks more harmony to be able to survive and prosper together.

Russia, on the other hand, seeks more influence and refuses to think in terms
of win-win globally.[6]

According to Yatsenuk's assessment of the conflict:

What's at stake today? The future of my country and the freedom of my people.
It's all about freedom. And we want to be very clear, we will never surrender.
We will do everything in order to save the country, in order to save my people
and in order to have my country as an independent one.

We heavily rely on the support of the Western world. And we do get this
support. And we do understand that it's up to Ukrainian people to shape our
future. The new Ukrainian government is ready to deliver changes. We are
ready to implement reforms. But you can't do it having Russian tanks and Russian soldiers on your soil.[7]

There is a sober and cerebral understanding that Ukraine has been undergoing the important and uneasy struggle of self-identification and nation building for the last twenty years. Moreover, the political leaders of Ukraine acknowledge the corrupt and contradictory political practices of the previous Ukrainian regimes, such as that of deposed president Yanukovich and his corrupt Party of Regions. During the 2016 Independence Day parade in Kyiv, President Proshenko said:

> We got lost in the arrows of the multi-vector policy trying to keep a foot in both camps. A constant lookback to Moscow and a belief in mythical brotherhood, paternalism and socialistic stereotypes firmly settled in the public conscience hampering the movement like weights on the legs. The political elite, in general, lagged behind instead of leading the way. For a long time, they were enchained by populist electoral addiction and mercantile vested interests, while their planning horizon did not cover the time after the next election campaign. This corporate sin has been accumulated by the elite for the two decades, and we—those who are in power now—are to redeem it before the people.[8]

The issue of the national sovereignty and territorial integrity of Ukraine is very poignant and pivotal issue for Ukrainian political leadership. Most politicians, from both governmental and opposition, speak about united multiethnic Ukraine, where linguistic and ethnic differences are not basis for political or socioeconomic discrimination. The Revolution of Dignity and subsequent Russian aggression are credited with fostering the catharsis of the nation-building process. During the parade to commemorate the twenty-fifth anniversary of Ukraine's impendence, Proshenko proclaimed:

> Ernest Renan, a famous French thinker, said that the nation means an everyday plebiscite. Since the very start of Russian aggression against Ukraine in February 2014, Ukrainians have been actively voting for united, independent, unitary, democratic, European Ukraine every day.
>
> The external threat accelerated the process of contemporary Ukrainian political nation building on the basis of civic patriotism. Ukrainian-speaking and Russian-speaking citizens as well as the citizens speaking other languages ... Ukrainians, ethnic Russians, Crimean Tatars, and other ethnic groups firmly uphold the position of Ukrainian patriotism. Shoulder to shoulder defend our state arms in hand.
>
> My separate greetings on the occasion of the Independence Day to Ukrainian patriots in the annexed Crimea and the occupied Donbas. My dear, we love you and try hard to have you returned to Ukraine. We are doing this by political diplomacy methods, because we care about you. This is the Kremlin who perceives your land as the theater of operations, and the region's civilians as cannon

fodder to satisfy their imperial appetite. While for us, you are ours, near and dear ones, temporarily separated from your Ukrainian family. The family which will definitely unite and meet at the festive table.[9]

The Ukrainian leadership sees cooperation with Europe and the United States as key in combating Russian aggression and ensuring the preservation of Ukrainian sovereignty. During the visit to Ukraine by the US secretary of state John Kerry, in a joint press conference President Proshenko said:

> For Ukrainians it is important to understand that the United States stands as a strategic partner alongside Ukraine against the challenges that are facing our country. And we hope that the American Government will also provide for the continuity of support of Ukraine.
>
> Ukraine expects that the Great Five and the Ukraine-NATO format will enable us to coordinate further, further forcing the Russian Federation to de-occupy the Crimea and the occupied territories in the east of Ukraine. And we have to find the international mechanism for de-occupation of Crimea. In this context, it is important for us to keep solidarity and mutual responsibility. Only thanks to this international responsibility for sanctions pressure against Russia can be provided.[10]

Yet, there are those in Verkhovna Rada of Ukraine who are critical of the appeasement rhetoric common among some European political elites. The leader of the Radical Party Oleg Lyashko, a colorful character in his own right, addressed those issues in his March 25, 2016, post on his official website.

> Meanwhile, in Europe there are many of those who are seeking peace at any price, and who are ready to yield to Putin for the economic benefits that it might bring to their countries. Their views are reflected by … the shameful and, above all, erroneous policy of appeasement of the aggressor, and stubbornly continue their attempts to satisfy Putin's appetites with small pieces of territory (Crimea) and political concessions on Ukraine's sovereignty, including the constitutional system of Ukraine (among them an autonomy of Donbas). Despite my natural outrage, I tirelessly try to debunk these illusions and futile hopes of Europeans. In particular, I try to explain that the only reason for Putin's interest in a constitutional autonomy of Donbas in Ukraine lies in keeping this region as a strong anchor that would tightly hold our country in the Kremlin's zone of influence and would allow him to control policy decisions in Ukraine. And most importantly, it will prevent the implementation by Ukrainians of their European civilizational choice. Should this plan fail, at any opportune moment Putin would launch another "referendum" for the separation of the autonomous Donbas from Ukraine and possibly its "return" to Russia. He would implement the scenario that for nearly 25 years was realized by the Crimean autonomy, and would move on to the next target of his expansion. In pursuit of peace on the basis of appeasement of the aggressor Europeans may benefit in the short term, but strategically

Europe will lose. This policy only shows weakness and readiness to cede to intimidation, and therefore encourages the aggressor to further action and fuels the potential for a great war in Europe. The desire of politicians in Europe ... "not to close the door for dialogue with Russia" actually gives Putin a chance to split the civilized world, to confuse everyone in his web of Goebbels lies, to weaken the unity of democratic countries and find a convenient opportunity for his next punch. Policy that is based on European illusions and concessions has already been costly for Ukraine, and will only become costlier further on. I have been trying and shall continue to try to bring this truth to our partners.[11]

Thus, Ukrainian political leadership holds that Russian Federation took illegal and aggressive steps in the wake of the Revolution of Dignity and deposition of Yunokovich in February 2013. They explain Russia's position toward Ukraine, as well as, other neighboring countries in the light of Vladimir Putin's authoritarian regime and its fear of democratic revolutions. Furthermore, they see Ukraine as a sovereign European nation ready for a democratic and transparent government firmly allied with Europe and the United States. When it comes to the politics of Russian Federation, popular and political trust are extremely low.

Economics and Institutions

It is widely believed that the Association Agreement with the European Union was the main reason for the civil and political unrest in Ukraine in 2013. While it is true that Yanokovich's decision not to sign the long anticipated agreement on November 21, 2013, prompted the first wave of peaceful protests in Kyiv's Independence Square, which became known as Euromaidan, the subsequent escalation of tensions between the government and the protesters were caused by increasing dissatisfaction and anger toward the government's decisions and the use of force (Aslund, 2015; Kuzio, 2015; Onuch, 2015).

Yet, the signing of the Association Agreement with European Union became an important part of the agenda of the new postrevolutionary government. While the economic benefits of association are seen as very important and are believed to be a possible solution to Ukraine's economic vows, it is evident that association with Europe means much more than mere economic well-being. Ukrainians increasingly talk about the "European values," which include democratic and transparent governance, end of corruption, and vibrant civil society holding elected leadership accountable.

The document that we will sign today is not just political and economic. It is a symbol of fate and unbreakable will. It is a tribute to people who gave their lives and health to make this moment happen. And it is the strongest reminder that today's Europe is and must be about people's determination to live in a better and fairer world.

It took Ukraine 7 long years to walk the terrible, thorny road towards the political association and economic integration with the EU. This road saw its ups and downs, but today, we are finally here. All Ukraine, including Crimea, is starting to be a member of the Association Agreement with the EU.[12]

In his televised program "Ten Minutes with Prime Minister," Yatsenuk said:

Dear Ukrainian families!

I congratulate you with the New Year 2016! ... For all of us it's the year of real European integration, access to the largest European market and our way to the great European family.

The Agreement on a free trade area between Ukraine and the European Union came into effect on January 1, 2016. This is the agreement for which millions of Ukrainians fought on the Maidan. That is the perspective for the Ukrainian economy to become competitive, strong, exemplary and the one that attracts investment from the European Union, creates jobs, trades freely with Europe and allows the Ukrainian businesses to develop and move forward.

What is a free trade zone? First of all, this is the duty-free sale of Ukrainian goods to Europe and European goods to Ukraine. This means competition that is a challenge for the domestic producer. But first of all—an opportunity for Ukrainian business to become stronger, more competitive and win new markets. ...

Now European citizens need no visas to cross the Ukrainian border. We are looking forward to a final decision of the EU on granting a visa free regime for Ukrainian citizens, because we are members of one big European space. We share the same values. We share the same principles. We respect the rights and freedoms of a man and citizen. We are guided solely by the rule of law. ...

First of all, European integration means common mentality, common consciousness, common culture and common education. ...

We still have a lot of work to do, difficult, but correct one aimed at helping Ukraine to become an EU member, at making our citizens feel as worthy members of the great European family. This is our joint work. Joint work of every citizen of the country, joint work of the Government and Parliament. Joint work of the whole Ukrainian nation, which is a European nation, because Ukraine is Europe.[13]

The fight against corruption and the fight for increased transparency and the streamlining of institutional accountability and effectiveness continue to be central to Ukrainian politics. The government has taken several decisive steps toward reforms aimed at restructuring law enforcement, promoting accountability and responsiveness of the bureaucracy, and taxation. The closer association with Europe is often seen as a catharsis for these reforms. The immediate effects of the reforms are not very popular because they challenge the status quo and introduce radical changes, including significant economic costs. This trend has been observed in other Easter European countries, where the governments had to make difficult choices by implementing the demands of the European Union. The Ukrainian government faces similar difficulties, thus, the normative promise of European values is the key legitimating factor for the reform package.

Sociocultural Values

Besides economic and institutional reforms, Ukraine faces a number of nation-building reforms. Among these are the less than uncontroversial reform on de-communization. The de-communization reform demands the removal of Soviet-era relics, including the renaming of streets and cities. The reforms are met with the mixed set of feelings.

Natalia Korolevska, an MP from the Opposition Block, had the following to say about the reforms on March 23, 2016:

> I often feel ashamed of our Parliament and the MPs solutions. It's a shame to see how monuments are being destroyed, streets, towns, and whole cities are renamed. We hereby waive our history. I believe that all these riots and inadequate solutions of the "orange" coalition are in the result of bad manners. They don't know their history; don't remember the feats and victories of the people. They don't remember the merit of present veterans, who in a few years, restoring the country from the destruction of war, building factories, cities and towns have made an enormous contribution to the development and future of our country. I believe that it is necessary to return the practice of Patriotic education of youth by teaching them the history of their country in order they could proudly and without hesitation say: "I am a citizen of Ukraine."[14]

Among other pressing issues for Ukraine are the relations between regions of Ukraine. Some believe that the regional differences are too severe and federalism is necessary. Like the MP from the Opposition Block Nikolay Skorik:

> Many people have realized this over a decade ago, so in 2004 there were plans to decentralize power. Today, however, these plans encounter resistance to the Central government, which does not want to lose authority. And the loss of Crimea and war in Donbass is largely the result of the fact that decentralization of power has not been carried out in time. This error should be corrected. Ukraine needs real decentralization, which will provide a compromise between regions and in society in general. And the main rule should be the postulate "all regions are equal." The adoption of the Constitution with equal and strong regions will eliminate the danger of separatism.[15]

Yet, others believe that differences within Ukraine are not between regions, but in the mentality of different generations. A Euromaidan activist and member of the Parliament, Mustafa Nayyem, wrote the following on his Facebook page on August 24, 2016:

> Today, they say that the country has two fronts—east, where there is a real war for independence and internal, in a peaceful area, where every day is unfolding struggle for reform and a new country.
>
> Meanwhile, if you think about it, these two fronts have always existed in our country, those who fought and those who sought; Some cleared the field for others to build on it the new, present and independent.
>
> Unfortunately, these forces rarely walked shoulder to shoulder. Often, torn by disagreements and ambitions, they came into the war of mutual destruction, playing into the hands of those who used the country for their own benefit, thus creating hundreds of thousands of citizens who lost faith and became disillusioned.
>
> I do not want to be dramatic, but I sincerely believe that during these 25 years, we—as a generation and the country as a whole—have matured, become wiser and more aware. We do not yet go hand in hand. But despite the fact that civil society and social institutions continue to torment each other by mutual distrust, we have learned to see the common goal and feel a shared responsibility.

The same Mustafa Nayyem in his post on August 30, 2016, wrote:

> Everything went wrong at a time when President Petro Poroshenko and Prime Minister Arseniy Yatsenyuk … invited to the negotiating table oligarchs and their allies. As a result, the main partner and the support of the authorities were not the people, but the old scheme, clans, groups and methods.
>
> Was there another way out? Yes, there was. Immediately after the Maidan there was a period when it was possible to cut the old elite from the access to public resources, to burn bridges with the previous system by enlisting the enormous public support. Yes, it would be a war; Yes, it would not be comfortable. … But it would be a completely different country, there would be a completely different support for power and reform.
>
> Sooner or later we will have to take things into our own hands. The main mistake of our generation—is the lack of understanding of our own strengths and capabilities. Do not wait, when something is going to be done by the president, prime minister or speaker. It is extremely important to see the right people in the system, the right structure, the institutions that arise, and maintaining them, combining them, to build a united front.
>
> But now it is important to not only go out to fight, but come up with suggestions and solutions to specific problems. We can no longer be observers in the process, we ourselves are responsible. … The main thing—not to be observers, not to wait for someone who will win.[16]

Nayyem speaks specifically to the generational maturation and the rising levels of activism and awareness among Ukrainian citizens, which were shown in the empirical section of this chapter. Postrevolutionary Ukraine has shown higher levels of civic engagement and political awareness and tremendous rise in patriotism, which the Russian observers see as nationalistic.

CONCLUSION

The purpose of this chapter was to shed light on the current conflict between Russia and Ukraine through the prism of differences in value-based systems and narratives in the countries' identities. The analysis indicates that while the Ukrainians and the Russians share a common basis in many of the value categories such as work, family, etc., there are important differences in the geopolitical attitudes, visions of country development, and attitudes to institutions, as well as in the cultural identities of the two countries. These differences can help explain the magnitude of the current conflict. We shall pick up with important conversation in our concluding chapter.

NOTES

1. Transparency International, 2014.
2. International Republican Institute, 2013.
3. Proshenko, 2016a.
4. Savchenko, 2016.
5. White House, 2014.
6. Proshenko, 2016b.
7. Atlantic Council, 2014.
8. Proshenko, 2016c.
9. Proshenko, 2016c.
10. U.S. Department of State, 2016.
11. Lyashko, 2016.
12. Proshenko, 2016d.
13. Yatsenuk, 2016.
14. Korolevska, 2016.
15. Skorik, 2016.
16. Nayyem, 2016.

Chapter 5

Social Networks in Russian-Ukrainian Conflict

While chapter 4 tried to explain the causes of the recent Russia-Ukraine conflict through value-based and generational perspectives, this chapter aims at analyze the effects of the conflict on social relationships between different generations of Russians and Ukrainians. In order to trace the evolution of the interaction across the border before and in the aftermath of the conflict, we examine two types of networks. First, we examine business networks between companies in the IT sector (that includes gaming, computer and mobile forensics, online products and services) and second, we examine social networks between general populations on a popular social network website vkontakte.

Network analysis is the widely preferred method for assessing the evolution and effectiveness of social communication as it helps to portray the whole system of interactions among network actors and to rigorously evaluate the degree to which and by whom information is exchanged in a network (Tanjasiri et al., 2007; Valente and Davis, 1999; Provan and Milward, 1995).

Network analysis provides statistical measures of intensity of interaction within a network and the degree to which all the actors of the network are involved in collaborations and have equal access to network exchanges and opportunities (Turkina and Postnikov, 2012).

BUSINESS NETWORKS IN IT INDUSTRY

The information technology industry was chosen as an empirical setting for this study due to a high degree of interfirm collaboration (Lundvall, 1992). This industry also exhibits a high geographic clustering of firms. This clustering is evidence of eternal sourcing of knowledge and cross-border cooperation. Dense linkages between clusters are an imporatnt chracteristic of this industry (Lundvall, 1992; Mansell and Wehn, 1998; Quah, 2000).

The IT industry is very dynamic and vibrant both in Ukraine and in Russia largely due to its human capital. Elance, the leading online freelance site, ranks Ukraine as the third best place in the world to find people with advanced technological skills.[1] At the same time, Russia is very successful in the IT field due to its world-class science programs in its higher education system: half of Russia's higher education students major in science, a higher percentage than in China, Japan, India, Europe, and the United States.[2] According to one World Bank study Russia has the third highest per capita concentration of scientists and engineers in the world.[3]

We also chose to particularly focus on companies in Kyiv and in Moscow to avoid regional biases (e.g., East of Ukraine is more Russophone, etc.). European Cluster Observatory shows strong location quotients for industrial clustering in IT industry both in Kyiv and in Moscow regions.[4] This implies that IT industry is advanced in these regions and there are different IT companies working in these regions.

Next, we use the data from the Kompass online resource[5] to compile the list of relevant companies in Moscow and in Kyiv. We sample 51 relevant companies in Kyiv and 69 companies in Moscow. Next, we measure the relationship between two companies on a binary basis (0-no interaction/relationship, 1-any interaction/relationship (partner, common project, client, buyer-supplier, joint venture, any minor interaction through an event such as exhibition, conference, etc.)). This kind of approach to measuring network ties is common in the analysis of interorganizational networks (Soh, 2003; Dyer and Singh, 1998). We measure interactions using all the publicly available information about the companies: annual reports, newsletters, local news, and a binary search on internet. Whenever possible, we also called the companies to double-check the linkages that we had identified. Once we build the overall network, some companies formed isolated clusters, so we excluded those from the analysis. The final fully connected network consists of 34 Russian and 35 Ukrainian companies.

The relational matrix was analyzed with UCINET and NETDRAW tools and techniques. Figure 5.1 presents the landscape of business interactions between Kyiv and Moscow IT firms prior the conflict. Figure 5.2 presents business interactions in the same network in 2014–early 2015. Figure 5.3 presents the most recent interactions in the same network in late 2015–2016.

The first diagram indicates that even though most of the cooperation occurs inside city-clusters (the network is segmented into two clusters the Russian and the Ukrainian one), p-value 0.009), there is also a high degree of cooperation (intercluster density 22%) between Russian and Ukrainian IT firms. At the same time, diagram 2 shows decreasing levels of cooperation between

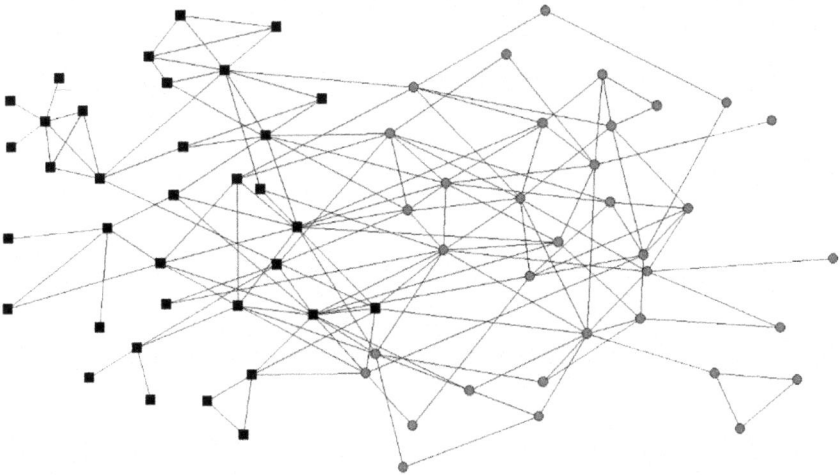

Figure 5.1   Interactions between Moscow IT Companies (circles) and Kyiv IT Companies (squares) in the Period 2012–2013. Created by the authors.

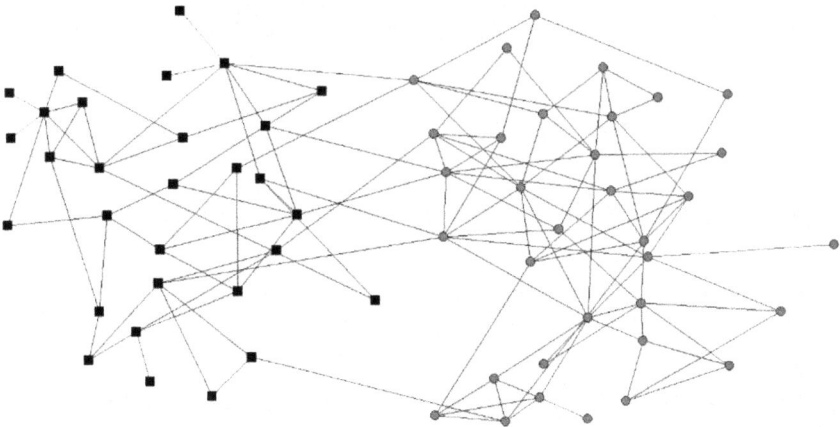

Figure 5.2   Interactions between Moscow IT Companies (circles) and Kyiv IT Companies (squares) in 2014–Early 2015. Created by the authors.

the two clusters (linkage density fell by more than 50%). In the second period too a few Ukrainian companies disappear from the network. The case-by-case analysis indicates that one firm reoriented its supply chains from the Ukrainian and Russian suppliers to Kazakh ones, two went out of business, and one disrupted its relations with the Russian partners, ceased its joint project with a Ukrainian company, and focused on new Ukrainian partners that are not part of this network. In the third period, however, we see the emergence

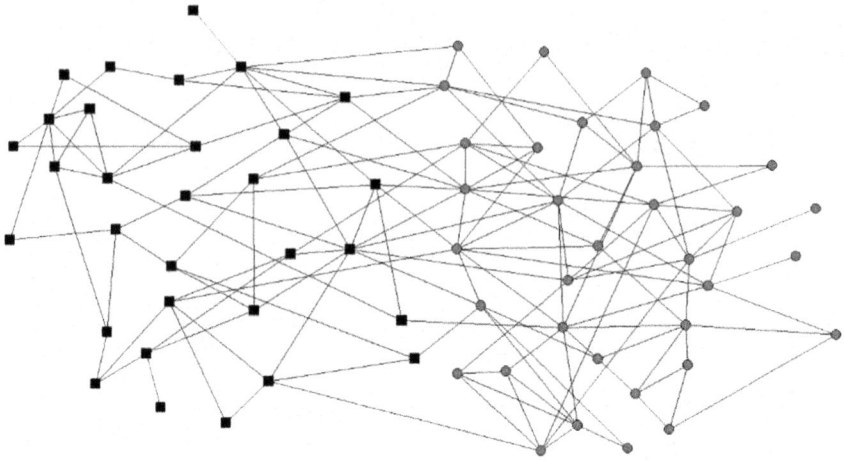

Figure 5.3   Interactions between Moscow IT Companies (circles) and Kyiv IT Companies (squares) in Late 2015–2016. Created by the authors.

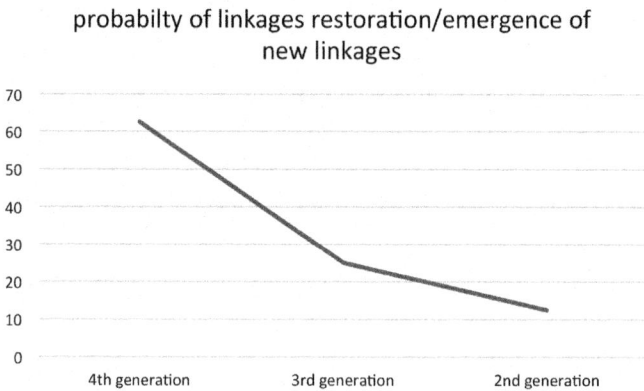

Figure 5.4   Probability of Restoration of Old Linkages or Emergence of New Linkages by CEO Belonging to Different Generations. Created by the authors.

of new linkages between the Russian and the Ukrainian network clusters and the return of some old linkages. Intercluster network density has increased by 36% from the second period, indicating that the linkages have gradually started to restore.

Generational analysis of linkages reveals that the lost linkages come back and new linkages in the latest period are formed between companies, whose CEOs are members of generation Y, or in other words, the fourth generation in our analysis. Figure 5.4 presents the probability of new links being formed or old links being restored by CEOs belonging to different generations. Note that in our sample there were no CEOs belonging to the first generation.

It is clear that the fourth generation is taking a much more proactive role in Russian-Ukrainian IT collaborations in the aftermath of the conflict. The analysis carried out in chapters 2 and 3 indicated that the members of generation 4 across different East European countries share some important commonalities: they are very individualistic, believe in democracy, are supportive of economic competition, and disapprove of state interference and state ownership. It appears that generation 4 is very pragmatic and business oriented. While political conflict had a temporary shocking effect on the network of interactions between the Russian and the Ukrainian companies run by the generation 4-CEOs, the linkages important for businesses on both sides became quickly restored and new linkages became created. Even though chapter 4 highlighted that the fourth generation of the Ukrainians is deeply dissatisfied with the country's institutions, does not trust the government, and is the strongest supporter of the Association Agreement with the European Union, all this does not prevent young Ukrainians from having a pragmatic approach with regard to partnering with their Russian counterparts when it comes to business interests.

ONLINE SOCIAL NETWORKING

In order to analyze the impact of the Russian-Ukrainian conflict on the general level of social networking and to model the online profiles of different generations, we analyzed several groups in a popular social networking website vkontakte where Russians and Ukrainians interact.[6] The following groups were analyzed: Славяне (134,998 members in September 2016) and ЭКОНОМИКА, ПОЛИТИКА, ОБЩЕСТВО, УПРАВЛЕНИЕ (34,918 members in September 2016) with more or less equal number of Russian and Ukrainian members. Analyzing the topics posted by members that gained popularity and collected many members for discussion, we analyzed profiles of those who posted the topics. We divided the topics into three broad categories: politics, economics, and culture (including leisure and hobbies). Figure 5.5 presents the probability of initiating a topic by belonging to different generations. Note that due to the lack of the members of the first generation, we did not include them into our analysis.

It is evident that different generations have very different online profiles. The fourth generation is the least interested in initiating political topics and is most interested in economics and culture-related topics. This finding should be interpreted with caution. The previous analysis of IT business networks demonstrated a considerable degree of pragmatism in young Ukrainians and Russians. Therefore, the lack of initiation of political topics in joint groups could be

PROBABILITY OF TOPIC INITIATION BY DIFFERENT
GENERATIONS

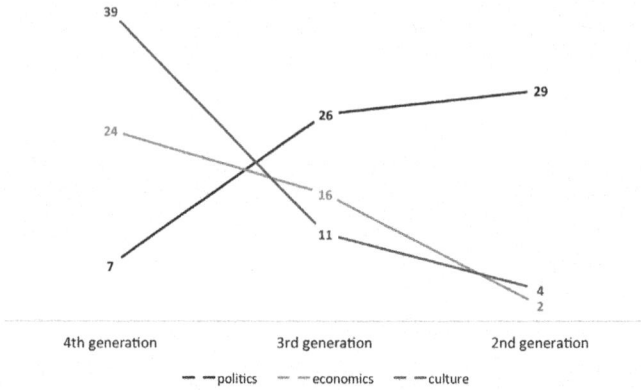

Figure 5.5   Probability of Topic Initiation by Generation. Created by the authors.

attributed to the planned pragmatic behavior by the generation Y to avoid open confrontation. The third generation tends to be in the middle (more interested in initiating political discussions than the first generation, but is also interested in culture and economics, even though to a lesser extent than the fourth generation), while the second generation tends to be very political in online social networking during the conflict. Additionally, we analyzed profiles of new members that joined the group during the conflict—they were mostly members of generation 4. At the same time, we also analyzed profiles of those who unsubscribed from the groups after a heated discussion under a topic posted, and those were mostly members of generation 3 and 2. It seems like generation 4 is more prone to keeping the dialogue and to going in-depth into sensitive discussions while keeping online linkages even in the case of large disagreements.

Similarly, we analyzed a convenience sample of online profiles of the members of 14 Russian-Ukrainian extended families including cousins and other relatives (using the same website vkontakte that gives detailed information on family members and gives access to their public profiles) and their behavioral patterns during the conflict. It is interesting that 21% of the members of generation 2 and 3 unfriended each other during the conflict and 6% restored the linkages in 2016. At the same time, only 4% of the members of generation 4 unfriended each other and all restored the linkages in 2016 except for one pair (two male cousins). These findings are very interesting given that in chapter 4 we demonstrated that the fourth generation of the Ukrainians is very dissatisfied with the country's institutions, does not trust the government, and does not see itself as part of the Common Wealth of

Independent States, and is more prone to participate in demonstrations than the other three generations, which can as well explain why the driving force behind the Maidan movement was the Ukrainian youth. At the same time, it seems like the Ukrainian youth are also willing to maintain a connection with their family members and social contacts in Russia and try to behave a-politically online, focusing more on economics-related and cultural issues in joint Russian-Ukrainian online groups.

Overall, these findings are compatible with our previous findings: generation fourth behaves in a more pragmatic way. One of our interviewees (member of the fourth generation and also a CEO of an IT start-up) in Ukraine mentioned:

> The worst thing we can do is to stop cross-border business and dialogue. While politicians are playing their dirty games, we will do common business and improve the economic wellbeing of our people. When I was confronted by the friends of my parents on why I am eager to do business with a Russian IT giant Kaspersky, I was truly impressed by their level of emotion. This is clearly the generation that does not care much about business, but more about their political sentiments about how the Russian government behaved during the conflict.

Another interviewee (top manager, small IT business in Kyiv, member of the fourth generation) argued:

> Youth in current Ukraine is a very interesting phenomenon full of contrasts. On the one hand we have all those nationalist movements like Pravy Sector who are extremely anti-Russian; on the other hand, the majority of our youth are very business-oriented, very pragmatic people. They perceive themselves as Europeans and wholeheartedly support Ukraine's rapprochement with the European Union (you know, the Association), at the same time, they are not against doing business with Russia. In fact, they would love to see Russia becoming more European too.

CONCLUSION

This chapter analyzed behavioral trends in different generations of the Russians and the Ukrainians during the Russia-Ukraine political conflict. The analysis revealed interesting patterns. Generation Y happened to be instrumental in maintaining different types of social cross-border linkages (business linkages, family linkages, online social linkages), restoring cross-border linkages, and creating new cross-border linkages. The previous chapters showed that the members of generation Y across different East European countries share a lot of commonalities such as independence, individualist thinking and values, support for democracy, market and competition, and a great deal of pragmatism, which really puts them in contrast with other generations. They were the first generation raised in a new socio-economic and political system, free from early on to choose their own career, to become social and business entrepreneurs. These deep commonalities may explain why despite the fact that (as demonstrated in this chapter) the Ukrainian generation Y is much more dissatisfied with country's institutions than the Russian generation Y and gravitates toward the European Union as a polity, while Russian generation Y feels more as part of the CIS unity, they are still able to find a common language and to create and re-create cross-border linkages.

Overall, these findings highlight once again the important generation gap in Eastern Europe that was produced by the marked changes of all the socio-political and economic structures following the collapse of the Soviet Union. At the same time, important commonalities in values in the members of generation Y across the post-communist space (even in the cases with some differences in geopolitical orientations) give hope for possible mediation and weakening of existing conflicts once the members of this generation progress to important decision-making positions.

NOTES

1. Greg Satell, "Could Ukraine be Next Silicone Valley?" Forbes, November 24, 2014. http://www.forbes.com/sites/gregsatell/2014/11/24/could-ukraine-be-the-next-silicon-valley/#4d9e62153eea

2. F. Joseph Dresen, "The growth of Russian IT outsourcing industry: the beginning of Russian economic diversification," Wilson Center, July 7, 2011. https://www.wilsoncenter.org/publication/the-growth-russias-it-outsourcing-industry-the-beginning-russian-economic

3. F. Joseph Dresen, "The growth of Russian IT outsourcing industry: the beginning of Russian economic diversification," Wilson Center, July 7, 2011.

4. Clusterobservatory.eu

5. Ua.kompass.com

6. Vk.com

Conclusion

Generation WhY?

The questions of "Fathers and Sons" is more than a prominent theme in Russian classical literature.[1] The generational conflicts occur in any society and prove to be both a puzzle and a rite of passage of every prospective generation. In the age of globalization, the younger generations experience the world in a different way than do their parents and grandparents due to the rapidly developing and ever-changing reality of their surroundings. The older generations often find it difficult to relate to the younger generations. Yet, as every generation comes of age, it leaves an impact on societal structures as a whole. From "baby boomers" to "millennials," societal norms and values transform in new and unexpected ways.

The existing literature on social change credits these changes in values and attitudes to two mechanisms: cohort replacement and intra-cohort change (Firebaugh, 1997). The first mechanism relies on the assumption that values and attitudes are formed during the socialization period and remain stable as person ages (Danigelis, Hardy, & Cutler, 2007; Mannheim, 1952a). The second mechanism suggests that values are influenced by life-cycle changes and therefore can change as person ages and experiences life. Thus, according to the cohort replacement approach, the intergenerational divergences are inevitable, variable, and most importantly stable, depending on the context which shaped the values of different generations. The intra-cohort mechanism, on the other hand, suggests that significant sociopolitical events will influence all generations, thus intergenerational convergences of values are more likely.

The profound effects of postcommunist transitions on domestic audiences of post-Soviet societies are well documented in literature. Coupled with the transformational forces of globalization, the postcommunist transition challenged the existing politico-economic regimes and territorial boundaries. This led to a diffusion of resources, norms, and values across borders and had a significant impact on people's values, beliefs, and perceptions. While there have been studies that explored the effects of postcommunist transition on people's norms, beliefs, and perceptions (Reisinger, Miller, Hesli, & Maher, 1994), few analyses focused on norms and values from the generations' gap perspective.

The analysis presented in this book sought to explore the so-called "generational conflict" which was brought into a sharp relief by the transitional experience. We pay special attention to the generation whose socialization period—the term widely used in sociological and socio-psychological literature to denote teenage years (Mishler & Rose, 2007; Searing, Schwartz, & Lind, 1973)—coincided with the period of political transition in the wake of the collapse of the Soviet Union. The special focus on the transitional generation is intentional. The persons who were teens during the politico-economic transition of late 1980s and 1990s are now approaching the productive and politically active decades of their lives. We called this generation— "Generation WhY." As we hypothesized, the transitional period following the collapse of the Soviet Union has had a profound impact on all generations, yet it set apart the representatives of the "Generation WhY." As predicted by the cohort replacement approach, the contexts of the socialization period of this generation produced a number of seismic changes in norms and values which relate to economic and political relationships in these societies. Moreover, we see that the members of this generation also exhibit a potential for a dramatic shift in cultural values deviating from traditional norms.

Yet, the years of the transition were not the same in all of the successor states of the Soviet Union. It is therefore, not surprising that interstate variation between the member of the "Generation WhY" as well as general degree of variability of intergenerational conflict will differ among the newly independent states.

A conflict between Ukraine and Russia is recognized as one of the most significant among the conflict in the post-Soviet space in the beginning of the twenty-first century. It has been suggested that the conflict is a direct result of postcommunist transition and the changes in societal experiences and values in the last twenty years (Kuzio, 2015; Riabchuk, 2015). Yet, the empirical evidence of these assertions is rather weak. The analysis presented in this book's chapters offered a unique and rigorous study, which focused on elucidating the effects of politico-economic regime change on the socio-economic and political values among transitional societies. Moreover, we sought to explore these interstate and intergenerational differences as a possible explanation for the ongoing conflict between Russia and Ukraine.

It has been suggested that the main source of conflict, which originated in the wake of anti-government protests, Euromaidan, in Ukraine in late 2013 early 2014, is a civilizational choice between Europe/West and Russia.

Ukraine is perceived as a divided nation split in its choice of the future geo-political vector. Furthermore, these choices are frequently tied to the regional and ethno-linguistic variation in Ukraine. Yet, our analysis suggests that the story is much more nuanced. Over the last twenty years both societies have undergone several important, but not at all similar transformational processes, which shook up the Soviet models of internal and mutual self-identification. In Ukraine, where national identity was very weak in the 1990s, the new post-soviet generation does not identify with old structures of the Soviet Union. Moreover, the cynical corruption of the previous regime left the popula-tion, particularly the members of the "Generation WhY" with disgust and few options but to change the system to encourage more transparency and accountability. While the European Union serves as an important and mean-ingful source of galvanization of these prodemocratic attitudes, it is not the main source of them. We find that the Russian and Ukrainian public, while share some important similarities in cultural values, have a very different set of political and economic attitudes. Yet, our findings also suggest that the members of the Generation "WhY" in both countries exhibit a convergence of values. They share similar characteristics of individualism, pragmatism, distaste for corruption, and preference for institutional transparency.

GENERATION WHY?: POST-SOVIET TRANSITION IN THE SOVIET UNION

While the so-called generational conflict is present in all societies, the analy-sis presented in this book sought to highlight the effects of economic and political transition on postcommunist Europe. It is generally assumed that generations that are closer to each other are supposed to have higher conver-gence of norms, ideals, and beliefs than generations further apart from each other. However, some studies find that there can be turning points among generations and even generations that are close to each other might have significant differences in norms, values, perceptions, and life (e.g., Strauss & Howe, 1991). In the preceding chapters, we have argued that postcommunist transition, which followed the collapse of the Soviet Union, was one such momentous turning point.

The last generation of Soviet citizens, whom we dubbed "Generation WhY," simultaneously experienced the socialization into the withering albeit institutionalized socialist state, liberalization of the last decade of the Soviet Union, and the postcommunist transition and became very different from the previous generations that were raised during the Soviet times. Building on the theoretical foundation of "generational conflict" developed by Karl Mannheim (1952b) and developed by a series of sociologists (Alwin &

Ryan, 2003; Dunham, 1998; Turner & Edmunds, 2002), our analysis have consistently shown that the generation whose socialization period coincide with the postcommunist transition developed a set of values much different from their parents and grandparents. Our findings suggest that contrary to the expectation of accepted sociological theories, people of different generations yet socialized under the same sociopolitical system have more in common with each other than those folks who were socialized during the period of politico-economic transition.

As discussed in detail in the preceding chapters, the post-Soviet transition gave rise to many individualistic and *adventurist* features which were completely nontypical of collective Soviet society. It increased the level of self-consciousness, self-reliance, and independence in a younger generation. At the same time, the transition period of the early 1990s created a certain fascination and admiration for the Western-type lifestyle and system of values. Harsh economic conditions, social and political degradation, and new realities enabled young people to mature very fast and evaluate the lives and experiences of their parents and those of their own through the prism of the major transition of the politico-economic system, which was not only about politics and economics, but also largely about the way of thinking and perceiving life.

Thus, it is not surprising that with the influx of new opportunities granted by increased mobility and market relations within and between the post-Soviet societies and outside world, the new generation of post-Soviet citizens have come to cultivate a new set of norms and expectations for their relationship among themselves and governing institutions.

DOMESTIC VALUES AND FOREIGN POLICY DECISIONS

The constructivist approach to international relations suggests that societal values influence the domestic and foreign policy choices of the state. Adopting these approach, the preceding chapters have argued that current politico-economic trajectories pursued by the postcommunist Europe are influenced by the value systems developed over the last twenty years.

Constructivist literature emphasizes the fact that trust, collaboration, and politico-economic integration between states are possible when they identify with each other. When states as social actors do not identify with each other within the existing social structure, there will be revisionist and even revolutionary efforts that will lead to a conflict, the result of which will be a significant change in the social structure (Wendt, 1995, 2001)

In the landscape of international relations of the post-Soviet arena, there are important re-identification processes which have been taking shape over the last twenty years. A new national consciousness is constructed by contrasting the values of the East European countries with those of Russia and through emphasizing the belonging of the Central and Eastern European countries to the Western civilization and Western institutions such as the European Union and /or NATO and the United States. Moreover, there are cross-national variations in the new national consciousness with the strongest in the Baltic states to the weakest in Belarus (Fofanova & Morozov, 2009; Morozov, 2009).

The analysis presented in the preceding chapters highlights these differences vividly. The nation-building projects are closely related to the questioning or full demolition of the previous Soviet identities. The members of the Generation "WhY" are less and less familiar with the Soviet identity and mythos of fraternal solidarity that existed under previous regime. As our analysis shows, coming of age in the newly independent nation-states, the new generation of post-Soviet citizens are more likely to display strong national identities. Moreover, the prospect of a closer union with Europe is strong among the members of this generation, due in large part to the newly found freedom of personal mobility and cross border communication, albeit country variations persist.

Inglehart and Welzel predicted that over time with economic growth and modernization all the generations in postcommunist societies will gradually shift toward postmodern emancipatory values (2005). Our analysis split the values into three interrelated categories of economic, political, and cultural attitudes and predicted that economic and political shift will take place first with the deep cultural changes to follow. The results presented in the preceding chapters support these assertions. We further find that political and economic proximity to the European Union foster harmonization of generational gaps as well as serves as catharsis for emancipatory postmodern values. Thus, the soft power of the European Union continues to shape politics in its neighborhood in a very meaningful way.

EUROPEAN UNION AND DOMESTIC VALUE CHANGES

The research focusing on the accession to the European Union and its effects on the Central and Eastern European states highlights numerous areas of domestic politics, economics, and society where European Union's influences are highly visible and tangible (Bafoil, 2009; Grabbe, 2002, 2006; Schimmelfennig, 2003; Schimmelfennig, Engert, & Knobel, 2006; Schimmelfennig & Sedelmeier, 2005). For instance, the development of functioning market economies presented a serious challenge for postcommunist societies. Given that these new states had very little if any experience with a market

economy, the European Union has been instrumental in fostering the transformation (Bafoil, 2009; Iankova, 2002). Furthermore, the conditionality of
accession directly influenced the flow and content of domestic public policy
shaping the institutional and legal structures of the candidate states (Cerami,
2008). The conditionality of accession has also brought changes into the
social policies of Eastern European states. Inclusion of minorities, legal protection of human rights and environmental awareness were the main areas of
focus (Krizsan & Popa, 2010).

We agree with previous research suggesting that accession has also functioned as a vehicle for disseminating ideas and transferring norms (Ekiert,
Kubik, & Vachudova, 2007; O'Dwyer, 2012; Vachudova, 2005). As Olson
(2002) points out, the word *Europe* has taken on an important political implication. Europe is no longer perceived as a mere geographic entity. It refers
to certain set of institutions, policies and, most importantly, values. These
sentiments are echoed in the finding of the chapters 2 and 3.

Our analysis in chapter 2 clearly shows that accession to the European
Union served as a harmonizing effect on intergeneration conflict in the
new member states. Central and Eastern European countries that became
EU members show a trend of convergence in politico-economic values
with EU-15 countries. The European Union also appeared to show some
harmonizing power on intergenerational frictions in the countries with EU
membership prospects. In countries that did not join the European Union and
which, therefore, lacked a strong consolidating mechanism to pull the society together, the transition to a market economy and integration of domestic
economies into the common market system and new sociopolitical realities
created considerable intergenerational frictions. These societies also lacked
good policy and economic models and considerable assistance and guidance
in the establishment of the new regime.

In recent decades, Ukraine has sought to move toward closer relationship
with the European Union. We tested the influence of the European Union on
domestic values in Ukraine by analyzing the attitudes toward the rights of
sexual minorities in chapter 3. The rights of sexual minorities are often seen
as challenging the traditional morality of societies and therefore have historically been under the purview of domestic politics. In the last few years, however, the European Union has taken very determined steps toward regulation
of these arenas. The subject of homosexuality in Ukraine was a moral taboo
during the Soviet era and remained as such during the years of democratic
transition. Homosexuality is often thought of as morally reprehensible and a
challenge to the traditional patriarchal family structure.

Supranational institutions face a significant opportunity to help shape attitudes
on controversial issues in the EU neighborhood. However, our analysis shows
that supranational institutions reinforce or galvanize these attitudes primarily

among persons who already possess higher levels of supranational identity and emancipatory values. As we have seen from the previous chapters this identity is strongest among the member of the generation "WhY." This seems to suggest that if Ukraine continues on the trajectory of closer relations with the European Union more shifts in domestic value system of Ukraine are possible.

IDENTITIES, VALUES, AND THE RUSSIAN-UKRAINIAN CONFLICT

Value Differences

The conflict between Ukraine and Russia is a horrifying and sobering reality. For many Russians and Ukrainians, who believe in the fraternal relationship of these two nations, the conflict was unimaginable, even when armed "green men" occupied Crimea in March of 2014. For others, the conflict is an inevitable extension of what Anatol Lieven called "fraternal rivalry" (Lieven, 1999).

In our analysis presented in chapters 4 and 5, we find that while Russian and Ukrainian citizens share some deep cultural similarities, they have nonetheless very different attitudes about economics and political processes. Ukrainians appear to be more politically active than Russians (they give higher scores on questions related to signing petitions, participating in demonstrations, joining boycotts, etc.), they are also more often members of different organizations, including civil society organizations, and are generally less satisfied with the government and country's institutions than their Russian counterparts. Therefore, before the start of the conflict, the Ukrainians had been generally more prone to revolutionary actions than the Russians.

At the time of the survey, the Ukrainians did not see themselves as part of a nation as much as the Russians did, which might serve as an explanation for the regional divide between the East and the West of Ukraine and secessionist tendencies in Eastern Ukraine in the aftermath of the revolution. Yet, it is also evident that in the wake to the Crimean occupation and ongoing conflict with the Russian Federation, there is a shift in the direction of a more unified Ukrainian national identity. This is particularly evident among the members of the "Generation WhY," who grew up in the single independent Ukraine and take the territorial boundary and sovereignty of Ukraine for granted. Furthermore, the priorities of national aims of the two countries are rather different. At the time of the survey, Ukrainians were more preoccupied with economic growth and are generally less concerned with the necessity of having strong defence, unlike the Russian public. Yet, this is also changing since 2014, as Ukraine is building up its military and defence forces.

According to the results of our quantitative analysis in chapter 4, both Russians and Ukrainians view democracy as beneficial and necessary for the country's development. Yet, Ukrainians have felt over time that their government and institutions are increasingly nonrepresentative of the peoples' needs. We find especially that the members of generation "WhY" of the Ukrainians are very dissatisfied with the country's institutions, do not trust the government, do not see themselves as part of the Commonwealth of Independent States, and are more prone to participate in demonstrations than the other three generations. Thus, it should not come as surprise that this new generation of post-Soviet Ukrainians were active in mobilizing and executing the antiregime revolution as well as carry a new patriotic or in some cases nationalistic identity.

Identity Conflict

The issues of nationalism and national identity has been a prominent feature of the current conflict between Ukraine and Russia. From the start of the Euromaidan protests the Russian press has painted the events as an uprising fuelled by the right-wing nationalistic forces in Ukraine, such as Svoboda party and its militant wing the Right Sector. During the height of the revolution the Russian media and officials portrayed the events in Ukraine as a revival of fascism aimed at the extermination of the ethnically Russian and Russian speaking population of Ukraine. The occupation and annexation of Crimea were justified in such terms.

Indeed, the issues of identity are important for both states. For both Russia and Ukraine, the process of building the new post-Soviet identity has been a challenge. Ukraine, weary of the stigma of ethno-nationalism, struggled to build a unified national identity and the nation-building project often met with skepticism or opposition. For Russia, the national project proved just as challenging and full of ambiguity. Many of our respondents cited in chapter 4 mentioned the famous tensions between the Slavophils and the Westerners and spoke about other competing cultural narratives currently persevering in Russia: Russian Europeanness and Russia as a separate civilization. In both narratives Ukraine is very important. For Ukraine, on the other hand, Russia is just as important to the construction of the national narrative. From the Russian Empire to the Soviet Union, both nations have much to sort out.

The public support for Ukraine's pursuit of an European trajectory of development stirred concerns and fears among the Russian elite and some members of the population in both Ukraine and Russia. According to the survey conducted by the USAID, in 2013 48% of the Ukrainian population were supportive of the Association with the European Union. The European Union is generally viewed as a progressive democratic polity and there is a general perception in the countries in the neighborhood that European Union's institutions are effective and Europeanization has a positive politico-economic effects on the institutions in the neighborhood countries.

Yet, it is important to note that while the disappointment with the Yanukovych decision not to sign the association agreement with the European Union might have been the spark that started the civil unrest in Ukraine, the Revolution in Ukraine was a result of general dissatisfaction and increased anger with the Yanukovych government (Åslund, 2014; Kuzio, 2015; Onuch, 2015; Surzhko-Harned & Zahuranec, 2017). The precarious position of Ukraine locked in the conflict with Russia did not result entirely from Ukraine being caught in the middle of the geopolitical game of West vs. Russia. Rather, as our findings suggest, it is also a position of crossroads between democratic and accountable form of governance and neo-Soviet style authoritarianism.

There is sober realization that Ukraine has a long and arduous road of reform ahead. There is a general agreement among Ukrainians that there is a need to build a multiethnic Ukraine, where linguistic and ethnic differences become the basis for political or socioeconomic discrimination. The Revolution of Dignity and subsequent Russian aggression are credited with fostering the catharsis of the nation-building process. It has been argued that differences in Ukraine are not between regions, but in mentality between generations. Analysis presented in this book supports this assertion. Post-revolutionary Ukraine has shown higher levels of civic engagement and political awareness and a tremendous rise in patriotism, which the Russian observers see as nationalistic, and while there are still generational differences present in Ukraine, the events of the last few years, including the conflict with Russia, might be the kind of event that can trigger the intra-cohort mechanism that might lead to the harmonization of intergenerational differences in Ukraine.

When it comes to Generation "WhY," we find them to be pragmatic and oriented toward conflict resolution. The trust for institutions and political elite is low on both sides. It seems that the representatives of the Generation "WhY" on both sides are most interested in the normalization of life in both countries though interpersonal and business relationships. Given that this generation does not hold strong emotional ties to Soviet ideologies and identities, we hope that the folks of this generation will be key to the future resolution of the present conflict.

NOTE

1. Ivan Turgenev. 1862. "Fathers and Sons."

Appendix A

"Our Generations" Interview Questionnaire

Table A.1   Our "Generations" Questionnaire

Name
Place of birth and place where you live
Gender

Please use these questions as guidelines. You can answer one of the following questions in the form of an essay or you can deal with all of them or you can focus on other issues as well.

1. Your most impressive memory in connection with the existence of Soviet Union
2. Your most impressive memory in connection with the fall of the Soviet Union
3. What do you remember about *"perestroika"*? Please describe your most difficult and most positive experience during *"perestroika"* period.
4. Please describe the funniest episode of your life during "perestroika" times.
5. Did you have any experience with crossing internal borders (for instance, when you traveled to your relatives who lived in another Soviet country)? What were your impressions and feelings?
6. What impressed you most of all when you first traveled abroad (to a foreign country)?
7. Please describe your color-feelings-taste associations in connection with "perestroika" period.

Appendix B

Descriptive Statistics on the Interviewees

Table B.1 Descriptive Statistics on the Interviewees

Number of interviewees	20
Gender	11 male, 9 female
Country/region of origin	5 from Ukraine (cities: Kyiv, Odessa, Lviv, and Chernivtsi), 3 from Belarus (cities: Minsk, Mahilyow, and Slutzk), 6 from Central Russia (cities: Moscow, Ryazan, Cheboksari, Kolomna, St Petersburg, Nizhny Novgorod), 2 from Siberian Russia (cities: Novosibirsk and Tomsk), 1 from Tatarstan (Russia), 2 from Far East Russia (cities: Vladivostok and Habarovsk), and 1 from the Caucasus Russia (city: Mahachkala).
Age	Mean: 32 years, standard deviation 4 years
Interview dates	May 31, 2009–September 2009 (specific dates: May 31; June 2, 5, 7, 17, 20, 22, 25; July 12, 13, 26, 27; August 16, 18; September 2, 3)
Who took the interviews	The authors of this manuscript
Sample selection	Random selection of first 350 individuals of suitable age using "age" search function on vkontakte social network (similar to facebook), 20 agreed to give interview (6% response rate)

Appendix C
World Values Survey Questions

Here is a list of qualities that children can be encouraged to learn at home. Which, if any, do you consider to be especially important? Please choose up to five! (Code five mentions at the maximum):

Table C.1   World Values Questions

	Mentioned	Not mentioned	
a029.	Independence	1	2
a030.	Hard work	1	2
a032.	Feeling of responsibility	1	2
a034.	Imagination	1	2
a035.	Tolerance and respect for other people	1	2
a038.	Thrift, saving money and things	1	2
a039.	Determination, perseverance	1	2
a040.	Religious faith	1	2
a041.	Unselfishness	1	2
a042.	Obedience	1	2

e117. I'm going to describe various types of political systems and ask what you think about each as a way of governing this country. For each one, would you say it is a very good, fairly good, fairly bad, or very bad way of governing this country?

0. Democracy is bad (fairly bad and very bad)

1. Democracy is good (very good and fairly good)

e035. Now I'd like you to tell me your views on various issues. How would you place your views on this scale? 1 means you agree completely with the statement on the left; 10 means you agree completely with the statement on the right; and if your views fall somewhere in between, you can choose any number in between. (Code one number for each issue):

0. Incomes should be made more equal

1. We need larger income differences as incentives for individual effort e036.

0. Private ownership of business and industry

1. Government ownership of business and industry should be increased should be increased

e037.

0. The government should take more responsibility to ensure that everyone is provided for

1. People should take more responsibility to provide for themselves.

Appendix D
Survey Protocol

INTRODUCTION

Thank you for agreeing to participate in these research studies. In what follows, you will respond to two separate short surveys about current social and political events in Ukraine. Separate instruction sets have been provided for each study, so you will know when you have completed one and have begun the other.

SURVEY 1 (I.E., PRE-TEST) INTRODUCTION AND INSTRUCTION SET

Survey 1: This survey is part of a small cross-national study of citizens' political beliefs in Europe. Please respond to all questions honestly and to the best of your ability. Keep in mind that there are no correct answers—what matters is your personal opinion. All responses are strictly confidential. Thank you for your participation.

PRE-TEST QUESTIONNAIRE

1 Supranational identity levels

Which of these geographical groups would you say you belong to first of all?

- Locality or town where you live
- Region of country where you live
- Ukraine

- Europe
- The world as a whole

2 Supranational identity levels part II

And secondly?
- Locality or town where you live
- Region of country where you live
- Ukraine
- Europe
- The world as a whole

3 Pre-test tolerance of homosexuality (Please rate the extent to which you would be bothered by having members of each of the following groups as neighbors)

(1 = very bothered; 5 = not bothered at all)
- Gypsies
- Emotionally unstable people
- Homosexuals

4 Trust in domestic and international institutions

Please rate the extent to which you personally trust the following:
(1 = do not trust at all; 5 = trust completely)
- National government
- National political parties
- The Ukrainian legal system
- The European Union
- The United Nations

5 Pre-test support for LGBT rights

How strongly do you agree or disagree with the following statement:
(1 = strongly disagree; 5 = strongly agree)
- Homosexual men and women in Ukraine should have the same legal rights as heterosexual citizens.

6 Frequency of political discussion (political interest/cognitive mobilization control)

When you get together with friends, family, or colleagues, would you say you discuss political matters frequently, occasionally, rarely, or never?

- (1 = never; 4 = frequently)

7 Church attendance (religiosity control)

Apart from weddings, funerals, and christenings, about how often do you attend religious services these days?
- More than once a week
- Once a week
- Once a month
- Christmas/Easter day/other specific holy days
- Once a year
- Less often
- Never/practically never.

SURVEY 1 (I.E., PRE-TEST) CONCLUSION

This survey has concluded. Your anonymous responses have been recorded successfully. Thank you very much for your participation.
Please click "Next" to proceed to the next online study.

SURVEY 2 (I.E., 0 MANIPULATION AND POST-TEST) INTRODUCTION

Survey 2: Thank you for agreeing to participate in this brief study. Please respond to all questions honestly and to the best of your ability. Keep in mind that there are no correct answers —what matters is your personal opinion. All responses are strictly confidential. Thank you for your attentive participation.

EXPERIMENTAL FRAMES

Immediately following the instruction set, respondents are randomly assigned to view one of three experimental vignettes—a pro-LGBT rights EU frame, a pro-LGBT rights domestic NGO frame and a control frame.

Lead-in for all frames

The following excerpt appeared in a recent Kiyv Post article. Please read the brief excerpt before answering the survey questions

EU FRAME

The European Commission has said in a written note that respect for LGBT rights is becoming a strong legal and moral norm in EU policymaking. The Commission cited article 21 of the European Charter on Fundamental Rights, which explicitly forbid discrimination on grounds of sexual orientation. "In many European countries, however, lesbian, gay, bisexual and transgender (LGBT) people face discrimination and harassment on a daily basis. Prejudices and misconceptions about homosexuality fuel intolerant attitudes and behavior towards this community," the statement continued. The European Commission urged European publics both within and outside the European Union to join the fight for LGBT equality and pledge to never engage in or support discrimination against homosexuals. (109 words)

DOMESTIC FRAME

A group of 22 Ukrainian nongovernmental organizations delivered the government a public letter today calling for increased respect for LGBT rights in Ukrainian policymaking. The activists also urged common citizens to speak out against homophobic bills pending in Ukraine's parliament and to condemn discrimination of homosexuals. "In Ukraine today, lesbian, gay, bisexual and transgender (LGBT) people face discrimination and harassment on a daily basis," the letter said. "Prejudices and misconceptions about homosexuality fuel intolerant attitudes and behavior towards this community." Domestic activists urged citizens around the country to join the fight for LGBT equality and pledge to never engage in or support discrimination against homosexuals. (Words: 105)

CONTROL FRAME

Raul Castro announced on Sunday that he will step down as Cuba's president in 2018 following a final five-year term, for the first time putting a date on the end of the Castro era. "This will be my last term," Castro said, his voice firm, shortly after National Assembly elected him to a second term. He tapped rising star Miguel Diaz-Canel as his top lieutenant and first in the line of succession. The 52-year-old Diaz-Canel is now a heartbeat from the presidency and has risen higher than any other Cuban official who didn't directly participate in the tumultuous days of the revolution. (101 words)

POST-TEST QUESTIONNAIRE

1 Knowledge of the European Union

Using the following scale, how much do you feel you know about the European Union, its policies, and its institutions?
- (1 = nothing at all; 5 = a great deal)

2 Demographics

How old are you?
  Are you male or female?
  - Male
  - Female
  What is the highest level of education you have completed?
  - No formal education
  - Some primary school
  - Completed primary school
  - Some high school
  - Completed high school
  - Some university
  - Completed university
  - Some post-graduate training
  - Completed post-graduate training

3 Post-test tolerance of homosexuality

Please tell us if homosexuality can always be justified, never be justified, or something in between:
(1 = never; 5 = always)

4 Post-test support for LGBT rights

How strongly do you agree or disagree with the following statement:
(1 = strongly disagree; 5 = strongly agree)
  - Homosexual marriages should be allowed in our country.

"DEBRIEFING" STATEMENT

This survey has concluded. Your anonymous responses have been recorded successfully.

Please note that some statements/policy initiatives ascribed to public individuals or institutions earlier in the survey may not be factual. The purpose of this study was to examine citizens' reactions to both factual and hypothetical public statements and policies. Some respondents were randomly assigned to read factual news while others saw fictitious ones. Your responses are greatly appreciated and we thank you once again for your time.

References

Alonso, Sonia, and Ruben Ruiz-Rufino. 2007. "Political Representation and Ethnic Conflict in New Democracies." *European Journal of Political Research* 46: 237–267.

Alwin, Duane F, and Ryan J. McCammon. 2003. "Generations, Cohorts, and Social Change." In *Handbook of the Life Course*, edited by Jeylan T. Mortimer and Michael J. Shanahan. New York: Kluwer Academic/Plenum Publishers.

Arel, Dominique. 2006. "Introduction: Theorizing the Politics of Cultural Identities in Russia and Ukraine." In *Rebounding identities: the politics of identity in Russia and Ukraine*, edited by Dominique Arel and Blair A. Ruble, 365. Baltimore: Johns Hopkins University Press.

Åslund, Anders. 2014. "Oligarchs, Corruption, and European Integration." *Journal of Democracy* 25(3): 64–73.

Atlantic Council, 2014. "Transcript: Discussion with Ukrainian Prime Minister Arseniy Yatsenyuk" March 13, 2014. http://www.atlanticcouncil.org/news/transcripts/transcript-discussion-with-ukrainian-prime-minister-arseniy-yatsenyuk

Ayoub, Phillip. M. 2013. "Cooperative transnationalism in contemporary Europe: Europeanization and political opportunities for LGBT mobilization in the European union." *European Journal of Political Research* 5(2): 279–310.

Ayoub, Phillip. M. 2014. "With Arms Wide Shut: Threat Perception, Norm Reception and Mobilized Resistance to LGBT Rights." *Journal of Human Rights* 13(3): 337–362.

Bachev, Hrabrin. 2008. "Post-communist transformation in Bulgaria – Implications for development of agricultural specialization and farming structures." Munich Personal RePEc Archive. Institute of Agricultural Economics. http://mpra.ub.uni-muenchen.de/7771/

Bafoil, François. 2009. *Central and Eastern Europe: Europeanization and Social Change.* New York: Palgrave Macmillan.

Bartlett, Will. 1996. "From Reform to Crisis: Economic Impacts of Secession, War and Sanctions in the Former Yugoslavia." In *Problems of Economic and Political*

Transformation in the Balkans, edited by Ian Jeffries and Alin Teodorescu, 151–172. New York: Pinter.

Baum, Mathew A. and Tim Groelling. 2010. "Reality Asserts Itself: Public Opinion on Iraq and the Elasticity of Reality." *International Organization* 64(3): 443–479.

Bennett, W. Lance. 1990. "Toward a Theory of Press□state Relations in the United States." *Journal of Communication* 40(2):103–127.

Bennett, W. Lance, Regina G. Lawrence, and Steven Livingston. 2007. *When the press fails: Political Power and the News Media from Iraq to Katrina.* Studies in Communication, Media, and Public Opinion. University of Chicago Press.

Berinsky, Adam J. 2009. *In Time of War: Understanding American Public Opinion from World War II to Iraq.* Chicago: The University of Chicago Press.

Berinsky, Adam, and Jaime N. Druckman. 2007. "The polls—Review Public Opinion Research and Support for the Iraq War." *Public Opinion Quarterly* 71:141.

Börzel, Tanja A. 1999. "Towards Convergence in Europe? Institutional Adaptation to Europeanization in Germany and Spain." *Journal of Common Market Studies* 39 (4): 573–96.

Börzel, Tanja A. 2001. *The Domestic Impact of Europe: Institutional Adaptation in Germany and Spain.* Cambridge: Cambridge University Press.

Brown, Chris. 2005. *Understanding International Relations.* Basingstoke: Palgrave Publishing.

Bulmer, Simon. and Martin Burch. 2001. "The 'Europeanization' of Central Government." In *The Rules of Integration: Institutionalist Approaches to the Study of Europe.* edited by Gerald Schneider and Mark Aspinwall, 73–96. Manchester: Manchester University Press.

Bunce, Valerie. 1999. "Political Economy of Post-socialism." *Slavic Review* 58(4): 754–794.

Burant, Stephen R. 1995. "Foreign Policy and National Identity: A Comparison of Ukraine and Belarus." *Europe-Asia Studies* 47 (7): 1125–44.

Cafaggi, Fabrizio, Olha O. Cherdnychenko, Marice Cremona, Kati Cseres, Lukasz Cerami, Alfio. 2008. "Europeanization and social policy in Central and Eastern Europe." *Européanisation,* edited by François Bafoil and Timm Beichelt, 137–168. D'Ouest en Est. Coll. Logiques Politiques, L'Harmattan: Paris

Checkel, Jeffrey. 2004. "Social Constructivisms in Global and European Politics." *Review of International Studies* 30 (2): 229–244.

Cooper, Joel. 2007. *Cognitive Dissonance: 50 years of a Classic Theory.* Thousand Oaks: Sage.

Cowles, Maria Green, James Caporaso, and Thomas Risse, eds. 2001. *Transforming Europe: Europeanization and Domestic Change.* Ithaca: Cornell University Press.

Danigelis, Nicholas L., Melissa Hardy, and Stephen J. Cutler. 2007. "Population Aging, Intracohort Aging, and Sociopolitical Attitudes." *American Sociological Review* 72: 812–830.

Della Porta, Donatella, and Manuela Ciani. 2007. "Europeanization from Below? Social Movements and Europe." *International Quarterly* 12(1):1–20.

Di Quirico, Roberto, ed. 2005. *Europeanisation and Democratization: Institutional Adaptation, Conditionality and Democratization in EU's Neighbor Countries.* Florence: European Press Academic Publishing.

Dresen, F. Joseph. July 7, 2011. "The growth of Russian IT Outsourcing Industry: The Beginning of Russian Economic Diversification." Wilson Center. https://www. wilsoncenter.org/publication/the-growth-russias-it-outsourcing-industry-the-beginning-russian-economic

Druckman, James N. 2001. "The Implications of Framing Effects for Citizen Competence." *Political Behavior* 23(3): 225–256.

Duch, Raymond M. 1995. "Economic Chaos and the Fragility of Democratic Transition in Former Communist Regimes." *The Journal of Politics* 57(1): 121–158.

Dunham, Charlotte Chorn. 1998. "Generation Units & the Life Course: A Sociological Perspective on Youth and the Anti-War Movement." *Journal of Political and Military Sociology* 26 (2):137–155.

Edmunds, June and Bryan S. Turner. 2002. *Generations, Culture and Society*. Buckingham: Open University Press.

Ekiert, Grzegorz, Jan Kubik, and Milada Anna Vachudova. 2007. "Democracy in the Post-Communist World: An Unending Quest?" *East European Politics & Societies* 21(1): 7–30.

Elliott, John E. 1997. "The Role of Institutional Change in Post-Communist Transition." *International Journal of Social Economics* 24(7): 859–872.

Enev, Todor. 2006. *Employment Policy in Post-communist Europe*. Paper presented at the Annual Meeting of the International Studies Association, Town & Country Resort and Convention Center, San Diego, California.

Esses, Victoria M., and John F. Dovidio. 2002. "The Role of Emotions in Determining Willingness to Engage in Intergroup Contact." *Personality and Social Psychology Bulletin* 28: 1202–1214.

Featherstone, Kevin, and Claudio Radaelli, eds. 2002. *The Politics of Europeanisation.*, Oxford: Oxford University Press.

Finifter, Ada W. 1996. "Attitudes toward individual responsibility and political reform in the former Soviet Union." *American Political Science Review* 90(1):138–152.

Finifter, Ada W., and Ellen Mickiewicz. 1992. "Redefining the Political System of the USSR: Mass Support for Political Change." *American Political Science Review* 86(4): 857–874.

Firebaugh Glenn. 1997. *Analyzing Repeated Surveys*. Quantitative Application in Social Sciences. Sage University Papers, CA: Thousand Oaks.

Fleron, Frederic J. 1996. "Post-Soviet Political Culture in Russia: An Assessment of Recent Empirical Investigations." *Europe-Asia Studies* 48(2): 225–260.

Fofanova, Elena and Viatcheslav Morozov. 2009. "Imperial Legacy and the Russian-Baltic Relations: From Conflicting Historical Narratives to a Foreign Policy Confrontation?" In *Identity and Foreign Policy: Baltic-Russian Relations and European Integration*, edited by Eiki Berg and Piret Ehin, 15–31. Farnham: Ashgate.

Gibson, James L., Raymond M. Duch, and Kent L.Tedin. 1992. "Democratic Values and the Transformation of the Soviet Union." *Journal of Politics* 54(2): 329–371.

Glinavos, Ioannis. 2010. *Neoliberalism and the Law in Post-Communist Transition: The Evolving Role of Law in Russia's Transition to Capitalism.* New York: Routledge.

Goetz, Klaus H. 2001. "European Integration and National Executives: A Cause in Search of an Effect." In *Europeanised Politics. European Integration and National Political Systems,* edited by K.H. Goetz and S. Hix, 211–231. London: Frank Cass.

Goetz, Klaus H., and Simon Hix. 2001. *Europeanized Politics? European Integration and National Political Systems*. New York: Frank Cass Publishers.

Gorywoda, Lukasz., Hans-Wolfgang Michlitz, and Karolina Podstawa. 2010. "Europeanization of Private Law in Central and Eastern Europe: Preliminary Findings and Research Agenda." European University Institute. http://hdl.handle.net/1814/14740

Grabbe, Heather. 2002. "Europeanisation Goes East: Power and Uncertainty in the EU Accession Process" in *The Politics of Europeanisation*, edited by K. Featherstone and C. Radaelli, 303–330. Oxford: Oxford University Press.

Grabbe, Heather. 2006. *The EU's Transformative Power: Europeanization through Conditionality in Central and Eastern Europe*. New York: Palgrave Macmillan.

Grusky, David. 1994. *Social Stratification: Class, Race and Gender in Sociological Perspective*. Boulder: Westview Press.

Habermas, Jurgen. 2003. "Toward a Cosmopolitan Europe." *Journal of Democracy* 14(4): 86–100. doi:10.1353/jod.2003.0077

Halman, Loek, and Malina Voicu. 2010. *Mapping Value Orientations in Central and Eastern Europe*. Leiden: Brill Academic Pub.

Hansen, Flemming S. 2006. "The EU and Ukraine: Rhetorical Entrapment?" *European Security* 15(2): 115–135.

Hayes, Danny, and Matt Guardino. 2011. "The Influence of Foreign Voices on US Public Opinion." *American Journal of Political Science* 55(4): 831–851.

Hooghe, Liesbet. and Gary Marks. "Europe's Crises and Political Contestation." Paper presented at the Conference, "Theory Meets Crisis," Robert Schuman Centre, EUI, June 30-July 1, 2016.

Hopf, Ted. 1998. "The Promise of Constructivism in International Relations Theory." *International Security* 23 (1): 170–200.

Howe, Niel, and William Strauss. 1991. *Generations: The of America's Future, 1584 to 2069*. New York: Harper Prennial.

Hrycak, Alexandra. 2006. "Foundation Feminism and the Articulation of Hybrid Feminisms in Post-Socialist Ukraine." *East European Politics and Society* 20(1): 69–100.

Humphrey, Caroline. 1991. "'Icebergs, Barter, and the Mafia in Provincial Russia." *Anthropology Today* 7(2) 8–13.

Humphrey, Caroline. 2002. *The Unmaking of Soviet Life: Everyday Economies After Socialism*. Ithaca: Cornell University Press.

Iankova, Elena A. 2002. *Eastern European Capitalism in the Making*. New York: Cambridge US.

Inglehart, Robert, and Christian Welzel. 2005. *Modernization, Cultural Change, and Democracy: The Human Development Sequence*. Cambridge: Cambridge University Press.

Inkeles, Alex, and Raymond Augustine Bauer. 1959. *The Soviet Citizen: Daily Life in a Totalitarian Society*. Cambridge: Harvard University Press.

International Republican Institute. 2013. "IRI Ukraine Survey: Ukrainians Positive about Association Agreement with the EU" http://www.iri.org/resource/iri-ukraine-survey-ukrainians-positive-about-association-agreement-eu.

Kennedy, Michael, D. 2002. *Cultural Formations of Post-communism: Emancipation, Transition, Nation and War.* Minneapolis: University of Minnesota Press.

King, Lawrence. 2001. *The Basic Features of Post-communist Capitalism in Eastern Europe: Firms in Hungary, the Czech Republic, and Slovakia.* Greenwood Publishing Group.

King, Lawrence. 2002. "Post-communist Divergence: A Comparative Analysis of the Transition to Capitalism in Poland and Russia." *Studies in Comparative International Development (SCID)*, 37(3): 3–34.

King, L., & Szelenyi, I. (2001). *The Basic Features of Postcommunist Capitalism in Eastern Europe and Assessing New Class Theory.* Westport, CT: Praeger Press.

Kitschelt, Herbert. 1992. "The Formation of Party Systems in East Central Europe." *Politics and Society* 20(1): 7–50.

Kitschelt, Herbert. 1995. "Formation of Party Cleavages in Post-Communist Democracies: Theoretical Propositions." *Party Politics* 1(4):447–472.

Kitschelt, Herbert. 2000. "Linkages between Citizens and Politicians in Democratic Polities." *Comparative Political Studies* 33(6/7): 845–879.

Kopstein, Jeffery, and David Reilly. 2000. "Geographic Diffusion and the Transformation of the Post-communist World." *World Politics*, 53(1), 1–17.

Kornai, Janos, Stephan Haggard, and Robert R. Kaufman. 2001. *Reforming the State: Fiscal and Welfare Reform in Post-socialist Countries.* Cambridge: Cambridge University Press.

Korolevska, Natalia. 2016. "The Problems of the Current Coalition are in the Results of Bad Manners." *Opposition Block.* 23 March 2016. http://opposition.org.ua/en/news/nataliya-korolevska-problemi-ninishno-koalici-v-nedovikhovanni.html/

Krasteva, Anna, and Francesco Privitera. 2006. *Democratization in Post-communist Transition Processes in the 1990s: Lights and Shadows.* Vol. 27. Longo, Ravenna.

Krizsan, Andrea and Raluca Popa. 2010. "Europeanization in Making Policies against Domestic Violence in Central and Eastern Europe." *Social Politics: International Studies in Gender, State and Society* 17(3): 379–406.

Kuzio, Taras. 2000. "The National Factor in Ukraine's Quadruple Transition." *Contemporary Politics* 6(2): 143–164.

Kuzio, Taras. 2008. "Comparative Perspectives on Communist Successor parties in Central-Eastern Europe and Eurasia." *Communist and Post-Communist Studies* 41:397–419.

Kuzio, Taras. 2015. "Competing Nationalism, Euromaidan, and the Russian-Ukrainian conflict." *Studies in Ethnicity and Nationalism* 15 (1):157–169.

Lankina, Tomila, and Lullit Getachew. 2006. "A Geographic Incremental Theory of Democratization: Territory, Aid and Democracy in Post-communist Regions." *World Politics* 58(4): 536–582.

Leconte, Cecile. 2008. "Opposing Integration on Matters of Social and Normative Preferences: A New Dimension of Political Contestation in the EU." *Journal of Common Market Studies* 46(5):1071–1091.

Ledeneva, Alena. 2004. "Ambiguity of Social Networks in Post-communist Contexts." (Economics Working Papers 48). Centre for the Study of Economic and Social Change in Europe, SSEES, UCL: London, UK.

Lieven, Anatol. 1999. *Ukraine & Russia: A Fraternal Rivalry*. Washington, DC: United States Institute of Peace Press.

Linz, Juan J., and Alfred C. Stepan. 1996. *Problems of Democratic Transition and Consolidaton: Southern Europe, South America, and Post-Communist Europe*. Baltimore: Johns Hopkins University Press.

Lundvall, Bengt-Ake. 1992. *National Systems of Innovation. Towards Theory of Innovation and Interactive Learning*. London: Pinter Publishers.

Lupia, Arthur, and Mathew D. McCubbins. 2000. "Representation or Abdication? How Citizens Use Institutions to Help Delegation Succeed." *European Journal of Political Research* 37(3):291–307.

Lyashko, Oleh. 2016. "On the policy of Illusion and Concessions Europe." March 25, 2016. http://liashko.ua/eng/general/5-on-the-policy-of-illusions-and-concessions-by-europe#sthash.u8WlCYdG.dpuf

Mannheim, Karl. 1952. *Collected Works of Karl Mannheim*. Vol. 5. Routledge, London.

Mannheim, Karl. 1997. *Collected Works of Karl Mannheim*. Vol. 5. London: Routledge.

Mansell, Robin, and Uta Wehn. 1998. *Knowledge Societies: Information Technology for Sustainable Development, United Nation.*, Oxford University Press.

Mansfield, Edward. D., and Jack Snyder. 1995. "Democratization and the Danger of War." *International Security* 20(1):5–38.

Mansfield, Edward. D., and Jack Snyder. 2002. "Democratic Transitions, Institutional Strength, and War." *International Organization* 56(2): 297–337.

Mansfield, Edward. D., and Jack Snyder. 2005. *Electing to Fight: Why Emerging Democracies Go to War*. Cambridge, MA: MIT Press.

Martsenyuk, Tamara. 2012. "The State of the LGBT Community and Homophobia in Ukraine." *Problem of Post-Communism* 59(2):51–62.

Miller, Joanne, and Jon A. Krosnick. 2000. "News Media Impact on the Ingredients of Presidential Evaluations: Politically Knowledgeable Citizens are Guided by a Trusted Source." *American Journal of Political Science* 44(2): 301–315.

Mishler, William, and Richard Rose. 2001a. "Comparing Regime Support in Non-democratic and Democratic Countries." *Democratization* 9(2):1–20.

Mishler, William, and Richard Rose. 2001b. "Political Support for Incomplete Democracies: Realist vs. Idealist Theories and Measures." *International Political Science Review / Revue internationale de science politique* 22:303–320.

Mishler, William, and Richard Rose. 2007. "Generation, Age, and Time: The Dynamics of Political Learning during Russia's Transformation." *American Journal of Political Science* 51(4): 822–834.

Morozov, Viatchslav. 2009. "Obsessed with Identity: The IR in Post-Soviet Russia." *Journal of International Relations and Development* 12(2):200–205.

Munro, Neil. 2007. "Which Way Does Ukraine Face? Popular Orientations Toward Russia and Western Europe." *Problems of Post-Communism* 54(6):43–58.

Nayyem, Mustafa. 2016. Facebook Post. August 30, 2016.

Norris, Pippa. 1999. *Critical citizens: Global support for democratic government*. Oxford, England; New York: Oxford University Press.

O'Dwyer, Conor. 2006. "Reforming Regional Governance in East Central Europe: Europeanization or Domestic Politics as Usual?" *Easter European Politics and Societies* 20 (2): 219–253.

O'Dwyer, Conor. 2012. "Does the EU Help or Hinder Gay-rights Movements in Post-communist Europe? The Case of Poland." *East European Politics and Society* 28(4): 332–352.

Olson, Johan. 2002. "The Many Faces of Europeanization." *Journal of Common Market Studies* 40(5): 921–952.

Onuch, Olga. 2015." Facebook Made Me Do It: Understanding: The EuroMaidan Protester 'Tool-Kit'." *Studies in Ethnicity and Nationalism* 15 (1): 170–184.

Papava, Vladimer. 2005. *Necroeconomics: The Political Economy of Post-Communist Capitalism.* New York: iUniverse, Inc.

Papava, Vladimer, and Vepkhia Chocheli. 2003. *Financial Globalization and Post-Communist Georgia.* New York, NY: iUniverse.

Petty, Richard and Duane T. Wegener. 1998. "Matching Versus Mismatching Attitude Functions: Implications for Scrutiny of Persuasive Messages." *Personality and Social Psychology Bulletin* 24(3):227–400.

Proshenko, Petro. 2016a. "President's address on the occasion of the second anniversary of resistance to Russian occupation of Crimea 26 February 2016—17:06" http://www.president.gov.ua/en/news/zvernennya-prezidenta-shodo-drugoyi-richnici-pochatku-sproti-36799

Proshenko, Petro. 2016b. "Statement by President at High-Level Leaders' Roundtable "Political Leadership to Prevent and End Conflicts (Istanbul) 23 May 2016—14:28" http://www.president.gov.ua/en/news/zvernennya-prezidenta-do-uchasnikiv-kruglogo-stolu-visokogo-37169

Proshenko, Petro. 2016c. "Speech of the President of Ukraine Petro Poroshenko at the Independence Parade 24 August 2016—10:43" http://www.president.gov.ua/en/news/vistup-prezidenta-ukrayini-pid-chas-paradu-nezalezhnosti-37949

Proshenko, Petro 2016.d. "Speech of the President at the ceremony of signing the Association Agreement between Ukraine and the European Union, 27 June 2014" http://www.president.gov.ua/en/news/vistup-prezidenta-na-ceremoniyi-pidpisannya-ugodi-pro-asocia-33096

Provan, Keith G., and H. Brinton Milward. 1995. "A Preliminary Theory of Interogranizational Network Effectiveness. A Comparative Study of 4 Community Mental-Health Systems." *Administrative Science Quarterly* 40(1):1–33.

Quah, Danny. 2000. "Internet Cluster Emergence." *European Economic Review* 44(4):1032–1044.

Radaelli, Claudio. 2000. "Whither Europeanization? Concept Stretching and Substantive Change." *European Integration online Papers (EIoP)* 4 (8): 1–25. http://eiop.or.at/eiop/pdf/2000-008.pdf

Radaelli, Claudio, eds. 2002. *The Politics of Europeanisation.* Oxford: Oxford University Press.

Reisinger, William. M., Arthur A. Miller, Vicki Hesli and Kristen Hill Maher. 1994. "Political Values in Russia, Ukraine and Lithuania: Sources and Implications for Democracy." *British Journal of Political Science* 24:183–223.

Riabchuk, Mykola. 2015. "'Two Ukraines' Reconsidered: The End of Ukrainian Ambivalence?" *Studies in Ethnicity and Nationalism* 15(1):138–156.

Rose, Richard, and William Mishler. 1998. "Negative and Positive Party Identification in Post-Communist Countries." *Electoral Studies* 17(2): 217–234.

Rose, Richard, William Mishler, and Neil Munro. 2006. *Russian Transformed: Developing Popular Support for a New Regime.* Cambridge; New York: Cambridge University Press.

Rosenau, James N. 1992. *Turbulence in World Politics: A Theory of Change and Continuity.* Princeton, NJ: Princeton University Press.

Rouigrok, Nel, and Wouter van Atteveldt. 2007. "Global Angling with a Local Angle: How US, British, and Dutch Newspapers Frame Global and Local Terrorist Attacks." *The International Journal of Press/Politics* 12(1): 68–90.

Saivetz, Carol, and Anthony Jones. 1994. *In Search of Pluralism: Soviet and Post-Soviet Politics.* Boulder, CO: Westview.

Sakwa, Richard. 2008. *Russian Politics and Society.* New York: Routledge.

Samokhvalov, Vsevolod. 2007. "Relations in the Russia-Ukraine-EU triangles: 'zero-sum game' or not?" *Occasional Paper,* n 68, European Institute for Security Studies, September1, 2007.

Satell, Greg. "Could Ukraine be Next Silicone Valley?" Forbes, November 24, 2014. http://www.forbes.com/sites/gregsatell/2014/11/24/could-ukraine-be-the-next-silicon-valley/#4d9e62153eea

Savchenko, Nadiya. 2016. "Ukrainian pilot's powerful speech in Russian court: Full text" *UAToday.* March 3, 2016. http://uatoday.tv/politics/112-nadiya-savchenko-s-emotional-speech-in-russian-court-603118.html

Schimmelfennig, Frank. 2001," The Community Trap: Liberal Norms, Rhetorical Action, and the Eastern Enlargement of the European Union." *International Organization* 55 (1): 47–80.

Schimmelfennig, Frank. 2003. *The EU, NATO and the Integration of Europe: Rules and Rhetoric.* Camberidge, UK; New York: Cambridge University Press.

Schimmelfennig, Frank, Stefan Engert and Heiko Knobel. 2006. *International Socialization in Europe : European Organizations, Political Conditionality and Democratic Change.* Basingstoke, UK; New York: Palgrave Macmillan.

Schimmelfennig, Frank, and Ulrich Sedelmeier. 2005. *The Europeanization of Central and Eastern Europe.* Ithaca, NY: Cornell University Press.

Schneider, Gerald, and Mark Aspinwall, ed. 2001. *The Rules of Integration. Institutionalist Approaches to the Study of Europe.* Manchester: Manchester University Press.

Schmitter, Phillippe C. 2001. "The Influence of the International Context upon the Choice of National Institutions and Policies in Neo-democracies." In *The International Dimensions of Democratization: Europe and the Americas,* edited by Lawrence Whitehead, 26–55. Oxford, UK: Oxford University Press.

Searing, Donald D., Joel J. Schwartz and Alden E. Lind. 1973. "The Structuring Principle: Political Socialization and Belief System." *American Political Science Review* 67(2): 415–432.

Sedelmeier, Ulrich. 2001, "Eastern Enlargement: Risk, Rationality, and Role-compliance." In *The State of the European Union. Vol. 5: Risk. Reform, Resistance, and Revival,* edited by M.G. Cowles and M. Smith, 164–185. Oxford: Oxford University Press.

Skorik, Nikolay. 2016. "The Adoption of the Constitution with Equal and Strong Regions will Eliminate the Dangers of Separatism." *Opposition Block.* 01 July 2016 http://opposition.org.ua/en/news/mikola-skorik-ukhvalennya-konstituci-z-rivnimi-i-silnimi-regionami-usune-nebezpeku-separatizmu.html

Snyder, Jack. L. 2000. *From Voting to Violence: Democratization and Nationalist Conflict.* New York: Norton.

Stepanenko, Victor. 2006. "Civil Society in Post-Soviet Ukraine: Civic Ethos in the Framework of Corrupted Sociality?" *East European Politics and Society* 20(4):571–597.

Stern, David. 2012. "Ukraine Takes Aim Against 'Gay Propaganda'. " *BBC News.* October 11, 2012.

Stiglitz, Joseph E. 2002. *Globalization and Its Discontents.* 1st ed. W.W. Norton & Company.

Strauss, Anselm L. 1987. *Qualitative Analysis for Social Scientists.* Cambridge: Cambridge University Press.

Strauss, William and Neil Howe. 1991. *Generations: The History of America's Future, 1584–2069.* New York: Morrow.

Surzhko-Harned, Lena and Andrew J. Zahuranec. 2017. "Framing the Revolution: The Role of Social Media in Ukraine's Euromaidan Movement." *Nationality Papers* 45(5): 758-779. doi: 10.1080/00905992.2017.1289162

Tanjasiri, Sora Park, Jacqueline H. Tran, Paula Healani Palmer and Thomas W. Valente. 2007. "Network Analysis of an Organizational Collaboration for Pacific Islander Cancer Control." *Journal of Health Care for the Poor and Underserved* 18(4):184–96.

Transparency International. 2014. "Transparency International: Corruption Perceptions Index 2014." https://www.transparency.org/cpi2014/results.

Turgenev, Ivan. 1862. *Fathers and Sons.* Oxford: Oxford University Press; green edition.

Turkina, Ekaterina, and Evegniy Postnikov. 2012. "Cross-Border Inter-Firm Networks in the European Union's Eastern Neighbourhood: Integration via Organizational Learning." *Journal of Common Market Studies* 50(4): 632–52.

Turkina, Ekaterina and Lena Surzhko-Harned, 2014. Generational Differences in Values in Central and Eastern Europe: The Effects of Politico-Economic Transition. *Journal of Common Market Studies.* 52(6): 1374–1397.

U.S. Department of State. 2016. "Remarks with Ukrainian President Petro Poroshenko during press conference with John Kerry in Kyiv July 7, 2016."

Vachudova, Milada. A. 2005. *Europe Undivided. Democracy, Leverage, and Integration After Communism.* Oxford: Oxford University Press.

Valente, Tomas, and Rebecca L. Davis. 1999. "Accelerating the Diffusion of Innovations Using Opinion Leaders." *Annals of the American Academy of Political and Social Science* 566: 55–67.

Wallace, Claire, and Rossalina Latcheva. 2006. "Economic Transformation Outside the Law: Corruption, Trust in Public Institutions and the Informal Economy in Transition Countries of Central and Eastern Europe." *Europe-Asia Studies* 58(1):81–102.

Wendt, Alexander. 1995. "Constructing International Politics." *International Security* 20(1):71–81.

Wendt, Alexander. 2001. "Driving with the Rearview Mirror: On the Rational Science of Institutional Design." *International Organization* 55(4):1019–1049.

Wesolowski, Wlodzimierz. 1994. "Post-communist Transition to Democracy: Conflicting Principles of Political Action and Change." *International Journal of Sociology* 24(2–3):21–44.

White House, The Press Center. 2014. "Remarks to the Press by Vice President Joe Biden and Ukrainian Prime Minister Arseniy Yatsenyuk April 22, 2014" https://www.whitehouse.gov/the-press-office/2014/04/22/remarks-press-vice-president-joe-biden-and-ukrainian-prime-minister-arse

White, Stephen. 2000. *Russia's New Politics: The Management of a Post-Communist Society.* Cambridge, UK: Cambridge University Press.

Yatsenuk, Arsen. 2016. "Ten minutes with the Prime Minister. Ukraine is Europe." Government Portal, Web-portal of the Government of Ukraine. January 4, 2016. http://www.kmu.gov.ua/control/en/publish/article?art_id=248786329&cat_id=244851734

Yeningun, Cuneyt. 2008. "EU's role on the Western Balkan Democratization," *ICBS paper.* International Conference on Balkan Studies.

Zaller, John. 1992. *The Nature and Origins of Mass Opinion.* Cambridge, UK; New York: Cambridge University Press.

Index

About the Authors

Lena Surzhko-Harned is an assistant teaching professor of political science at Penn State University, Behrend College. She received her PhD in Political Science from the Kenneth P. Dietrich School of Arts and Sciences at the University of Pittsburgh. Her primary research interests are in the fields of comparative politics, political behavior, social media and politics, democracy and democratization, nationalism and ethnicity, politics of the European Union, and politics of post-Soviet states. Her work is featured in publications such as *International Research Quarterly, Journal of Common Market Studies, European Political Science Review, Nations and Nationalism* and others. She serves on the editorial board of the *Studies of Ethnicity and Nationalism* and is a member of a number of professional organizations, including American Political Science Association, European Union Studies Association, and Association for the Study of Ethnicity and Nationalism.

Ekaterina Turkina holds a PhD in public and international affairs from the University of Pittsburgh, United States. She is associate professor at HEC Montreal and a holder of professorship in international business networks. Ekaterina is also an associate editor of *Journal of Small Business and Entrepreneurship, as well as a member of International Advisory Board of International Journal of Productivity Management and Assessment Technologies.* Her main research areas are sociocultural and politico-economic contexts in international business, innovation and interfirm networks, international entrepreneurship, and industrial clustering. She has published in *World Economy Journal, Journal of Business Venturing, Journal of Common Market Studies, Journal of Business Research, Journal of European Integration, Cross Cultural Management: an International Journal, Physica A: Statistical Mechanics and its Applications, International Journal of Computer Science* *and Network,* and other journals. She has written three books and was a recipient of several awards, including the Highly Commended Paper Award from the Journal of Enterprising Communities, Best Paper on EU Governance from the European Community Studies Association, and the U.S. State Department Young Leaders Fellowship. She has recently become a finalist for the Alan Rugman Most Promising Scholar Award that is given to the most talented scientists under the age of forty.

9 781498 531979